# What Readers Are Saying . . .

"Eric and Leslie's story is a real life fairy tale, an inspiration, and an example of God's faithfulness. They have proven that high standards and patience in the perfect will of God produce beautiful fruit. They have given me reason to believe and hope, once more, in His time."
**—Livia Stecker, 18**
**Colville, WA**

"The Ludy's book on their biblical courtship provides a realistic alternative to the dating game most of us know today."
**—Sean McNeil, 18**
**Student at Liberty University in VA**

"Eric and Leslie's story is proof that pure biblical romance is tangible and truly liberating. It also serves as a checkpoint and encouragement to those of us who have embarked on God's narrow road of waiting and have, for one reason or another, lost a bit of our absolute trust that if we delight ourselves in the Lord, He *will* give us the desires of our hearts!"
**—Ryan Gold, 21**
**Englewood, CO**

"It was with tearful eyes that I read *His Perfect Faithfulness*. I had heard about courtship before . . . but I had never heard anyone's testimony who had actually done it. Eric and Leslie's story was really encouraging!"
**—Meredith Jordan, 14**
**Colorado Springs, CO**

"This book has been an incredible encouragement and blessing to me. It has confirmed in my heart that my commitment to wait on God for my spouse (and not to date) will be rewarding and filled with God's creativity."
**—Molly Gold, 17**
**Englewood, CO**

# About the Authors

Eric and Leslie Ludy were married in December of 1994. In working closely with many young people, they have witnessed the tremendous pressures today's youth are facing and have developed a deep desire to share Christ's love and truth with them.

Through writing, speaking, and individual relationships they are endeavoring to challenge young people to live at a higher level of purity and commitment to the Lord. They share their testimony with the hope that it will be used by God to bring encouragement to youth. Eric and Leslie are now speaking at churches, youth meetings, and conferences around the country. They also compose songs and minister together through music.

Eric and Leslie currently reside in Longmont, Colorado. They are pursuing an education that will equip them for their long-range interest in medical missions as well as contribute to their effectiveness in writing and music for future ministry.

# HIS PERFECT FAITHFULNESS

## *The Story of Our Courtship*

### Eric & Leslie Ludy

**FAMILY FOUNDATIONS PUBLISHING**
Littleton, Colorado

His Perfect Faithfulness

Family Foundations Publishing
P.O. Box 320
Littleton, Colorado 80160

Library of Congress Catalog Card Number 95-80695

ISBN 1-881189-05-8

*Printed in the United States of America*

This book is dedicated
with love and gratitude
to our families,
our best friends,
who have loved us unconditionally
and made countless sacrifices
to enrich our lives.
Without them,
this story could never have happened.
To the Ludys:
Win, Barb, Krissy, and Mark;
and to the Runkles:
Rich, Janet, David, and John.
Words are not enough to thank you!
We love you!

*O* Lord, Thou art my God;
I will exalt Thee, I will give thanks to Thy name;
For Thou hast worked wonders,
Plans formed long ago, with perfect faithfulness.

—Isaiah 25:1 NASB

# Contents

# Acknowledgements

A special thanks to . . .
Marlene Bagnull, for her energetic vision and confidence of victory, for her expertise in editing and typesetting, for her encouragement and creativity which transformed a little booklet into a *book,* and for her undying devotion to see this project to the end.

To . . .
Mark Ludy, for his servant's heart and for his howling humor; for offering us his amazing artistic talents to use and abuse; for continuing to smile, even when smiling seemed humanly impossible.

And to . . .
Paul Verschoof and Craig Hill, for believing in this project enough to give it wings and provide it with strength to fly.

# FOREWORD

IN A DAY AND AGE of intense focus on short-term pleasure, gratification, and self-fulfillment, it is very refreshing and a rare delight to run across a young couple with a deep understanding of true love and real romance. Eric and Leslie Ludy are such a couple to whom God has given insight and wisdom far beyond their years.

I have known Leslie's family for close to a decade as Leslie was one of our children's favorite baby-sitters in her early teenage years. Even at that early age, I recognized that God had found in Leslie a young woman through whom He could paint a visible picture of His love and joy toward people. When I subsequently met Eric, I could see that God's picture was completed not in one individual alone, but rather in their relationship as man and woman.

Although *His Perfect Faithfulness* is indeed the story of love and romance between a young man and his bride-to-be, it is even more the story of God's love and faithfulness toward anyone who will let Him be God. Many young people think that to allow God to manage their relationships with the opposite sex would be boring, restrictive, unfulfilling, and socially devastating. Eric and Leslie, through their lives and their writing, have masterfully demonstrated that God's purpose in all of our lives is not to restrict or hinder our romantic or sexual pleasure, but rather to maximize our enjoyment of and to take us to the very pinnacle of love, fulfillment, excitement, and pleasure.

God brings us a marriage partner because He has a unique destiny for us as a married couple. Even more so than the pleasure of romance and love, there is no greater joy or fulfillment than finding and accomplishing as a couple the purpose for which you were created. Far from boring, the most exciting life you could ever live is the one that God has planned for you.

Some young people reading this book may think, "God could never do for me what He has done for Eric and Leslie. They haven't been through the things that I have experienced. They grew up in an ideal family with Christian parents who never divorced, got involved with drugs or alcohol, or abused their children in any way." While it is true that Eric and Leslie have been blessed with wonderful families, the relationship of love, romance, purpose, and fulfillment that Eric and Leslie now enjoy is not a result of their family background or past circumstances. It is rather a result of the personal choices they have made in response to God and their circumstances.

All of us have been hurt by others and have made foolish choices in the past. Don't let what you have done or what has been done to you in the past control the choices you make for your future. Your past abuse is not your present excuse! God loves you and wants to reveal His perfect faithfulness to you, too, if you will let Him.

*His Perfect Faithfulness* is not just a book for unmarried young people. This is a book to be enjoyed and treasured by young and old, married and unmarried alike. As you read it, you will be encouraged and delighted. I highly recommend this book to anyone.

Craig Hill
Pastor

# The Story

## of

## Our

## Courtship

# *Tears and a Smile*
## *Eric*

I remember writing a little poem to Leslie that she could open and read the morning of our wedding day. In it, I attempted to articulate my inexpressible excitement to enter into a lifelong covenant with her—to be one with her life and to finally kiss those lips I had known, from what had become a painful distance, for three amazing years.

We had both eagerly awaited the moment she would come to me at the side of her father, dressed in the purest white and bearing her bouquet of new life. The moment symbolized so very much between us—not only the joys of rewarded patience and prayer, but the hope of what we both anticipate with the breath of our very beings . . . the imminent, triumphant return of Christ for His sparkling Bride. It was a moment we had talked and prayed about for many months, desiring it not only to be a precious moment shared between us, but a profound revelation of our future Bridegroom's glorious return.

In the little poem I had given her, I had finished with the promise that when she came down the aisle, I would be waiting for her with tears and a smile. Well, there I stood at the head of the aisle on that unforgettable eve in December, awaiting my princess's entrance.

The Jewish trumpet sounded, and all rose to their feet. There, with such joy in my heart, I stood and wept. I could not see her yet, and I struggled to mold a smile into my convulsing face of tears. Tears and a smile I had promised Leslie, but if she entered now, she would see only tears.

I strained to physically express the joy in my heart for my princess would soon enter through the wreathed archway. Suddenly, at the very moment I saw my beautiful bride, God's indescribable peace poured out upon the candle-lit sanctuary. A smile creased my tear-moistened face.

To a tune Leslie had written a couple years prior that we had entitled the "Sunrise Song," I beckoned her with the words:

> The trumpet calls you, Radiant Bride.
> Dressed in the purest, most dazzling white,
> Cherish this moment bathed in starlight,
> Christ's beautiful princess shining so bright.
> Beautiful emerald eyes, come to me,
> O Radiant Bride.
> A father gives up his daughter tonight.
> O what a prize . . . my Radiant Bride!

The sanctuary was heavy with emotion, and God's smile seemed to bathe our souls with His pleasure. The drama of that night was etched upon our hearts by God's very finger emblazoning forever upon our minds the significance of obedience unto the will of our Lord. As Oswald Chambers powerfully proclaimed in *My Utmost for His Highest*,

> Whenever God's will is in the ascendent, all compulsion is gone. When we choose deliberately to obey Him, then He will tax the remotest star and the last grain of sand to assist us with all His almighty power.

Never will we forget His perfect faithfulness. The writing of this story is but a pile of stones erected for the purpose of remembering the glorious work of our faithful King. He promised . . . then He performed. This story is one of love . . . Christ's love for His own.

# Bad Pizza?!
## Eric

My heart skipped a beat when I saw my princess for the very first time. "Who was she?" I wondered, and then her face vanished from my mind. I lay on my back in the dark of the December night snuggled warmly under my navy blue comforter. I stared up into blackness which held the reflection of a cross on the wall beside my bed. The streetlights played with the shutters and etched a "T" which I witnessed every night before I closed my eyes. It reminded me each and every night to tell my Lord that I trusted Him. Tonight it held my boggled attention and served as a focal point for my deliberating mind.

"Did I eat something funny tonight? Come on, Eric! Don't take your wild imagination seriously. Don't put your trust in strange and unusual experiences," I quickly told myself. My mind raced with justifications as to why the face of this unknown girl should be thrown aside as just plain weird and of inconsequence.

Just a few minutes earlier I had been praying for my future wife as I tried always to do before I went to bed. I was of the persuasion that God had chosen a precious young lady just for my life. I also felt that if she truly was out there somewhere, I would ask God to mold her into a beautiful and virtuous woman and prepare her for my life. There was nothing really unusual about this night other than the fact that tonight I was not praying on my knees but flat on my back. As I was praying, my mind had drifted to wondering what this treasure would be like, where she could possibly be, and what she might look like.

15

A sudden picture, a dream-like snapshot, popped into my mind's eye, accompanied with a soft message. The words were not spoken aloud but impressed upon my heart. "Eric, this is your wife." Startled, I stared at the picture of redemption illuminating my otherwise black bedroom.

I truly enjoyed the thrilling thought of knowing my wife was somewhere out there in the vast scope of humanity. Was she in China, Switzerland, New York, down the street? Only God knew, and He wasn't letting me in on the big secret! Was she a redhead, a blonde, a brunette? I could only trust that God would pick her out to match just what He knew I would take delight in.

But what was this? This strange snapshot of a smiling brunette limited down the field of possibility quite a bit. To be honest, I didn't really believe that this was from God. Ironically I now feel God knew I probably wouldn't. I gave more credence to it being the work of bad pizza than a stroke of God's mighty providence.

My memory would revisit this strange scene many times in the future as I sought God's perfect and pleasing will for my life. One day I would see God's enormous fingerprints all over this dark December night lighted only with the symbol of His great love for my life.

3

## Sweet Sixteen
### Leslie

The crisp December night air gently blew my dark hair around my face. Wistfully, I sat down on a cold bench to wait for my friends' arrival. It was two days before my sixteenth birthday— something I had awaited as long as I could remember—and a group of my high school friends were taking me out for a night on the town to celebrate. I should have been excited. After all, sweet sixteen was what I had been looking forward to for years. Yet for some strange reason, my eagerness had faded into a sort of gloomy depression.

"Why should I be feeling this way?" I asked myself. There was no reasonable answer. I had everything I could want as a teenager: a wonderful family, a large circle of friends, good grades, and an endless variety of social activities to occupy my time. I had a date for most dances or parties and I was generally well liked by everyone. I was part of church youth groups and had high moral standards. Most of my friends professed Christianity, as did the young men I dated, and I was careful to never attend any wild parties or hang out with the "wrong" crowd. Now that I was approaching sixteen, it meant even more to look forward to—a driver's license, the prom, and storybook romances. These were things I had always dreamed of, and now they were actually about to become reality.

Yet somehow, on this evening of celebration, I could not shake off a lonely ache inside. A voice in my mind seemed to whisper to my heart, "Something in your life isn't right. You are wasting your time. There is more to life than dating and popularity, dances and parties. You are chasing after foolish dreams . . ."

A frown crept over my youthful features. The words penetrated deeply. Somewhere within my soul I knew they were true, but my mind did its utmost to chase away such thoughts with clever justifications.

"What could be wrong in my life? Aren't friends and boys and parties just a part of the high school experience? These are supposed to be the best years of my life! Can't I be allowed to enjoy them?"

My rather unpleasant meditations were abruptly interrupted by the sound of a noisy car pulling into the driveway. Its passengers, a lively group of girls, were peering out the windows, giggling and waving to me. I forced a smile and determined to put these troublesome thoughts behind me as I ran out to meet my friends. I would not let such reflections ruin my sixteenth birthday. Yet for the rest of the evening and on into the following weeks I was haunted by them.

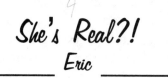

## She's Real?!
### Eric

Not thinking the strange experience a couple days before was from God rather muddled everything when again I saw this unknown brunette. This time her youthful features did not disappear.

I sat enjoying the beginning of a Christmas play at the church I had just begun to attend. A few days had passed, and my mind had long since forgotten the unusual picture that spoiled pizza had painted upon my mind—that is, until the unknown and mysterious brunette came waltzing out onto the stage.

My mind couldn't help but replay the short-lived drama of that dark December night. Again I felt a gentle voice impress upon my heart, "Eric, this is your wife."

"Now wait a minute!" My mind felt for its emergency brake and yanked it up. I didn't know the first thing about this young lady. Fighting to keep my thoughts in order with what would be pleasing to God, I quickly took that strange thought captive and attempted to enjoy the remainder of the play. But whether I wanted to or not, in some inquisitive chamber of my heart, I secretly took notice of this young lady's poise and dignity as well as her beautiful features that seemed to glow as she sang.

As a young man, I constantly battled with my thought life, and keeping it pure was a tireless struggle. I honestly thought that this was either a work of my own imagination or a cunning deception of the enemy. Therefore, I grappled to take this dangererous thought captive to the will of Christ Jesus.

God had been teaching me about the purity that He desired in my innermost parts. He'd been gently showing me it really didn't matter what purity I held externally if, in my thought life, I was given over to the lusts of my flesh. I had a growing desire to save not only my external body for my wife but also my emotions. I surely was not going to give any vain consideration to this unknown brunette just because of a strange coincidence.

At the conclusion of the play, I left my seat assured that this was not the work of God but a mere test to see if my loyalty was still with my Lord. This was aided in a most potent way when I met this smiling brunette just following the program. On stage she had appeared much taller as she stood next to young children and much older due to the virtues of stage make-up. But this talented actress was immediately and thoroughly omitted as a potential wife-to-be as I discovered, with my twenty-year-old mouth ajar, that she was only fifteen years old! "Obviously, this coincidence wasn't from God," my logical mind instantly concluded. Yet God would never let me forget it.

# The Dark Young Stranger
## _____ Leslie _____

I didn't really want to be in the Christmas musical. The cast was made up primarily of young children, and there was nobody else my age in it. Our church was small and did not have an abundance of people who were involved in drama or music so somehow, despite my lack of enthusiasm, I got stuck with the lead. I enjoyed acting and singing, but this little church play was not my definition of "cool." Worse yet, the performance was the night before my sixteenth birthday. Since I had little choice in the matter, however, I determined to make the most of it and arrived at the church an hour early to have my stage make-up applied.

As I prepared to walk out on stage, I caught a glimpse of two high school friends seating themselves in the front row. They were there to support me, I knew, but I was rather embarrassed to be seen in a church play with a bunch of little kids. The fact that I felt ashamed bothered me. "Why do I care so much what my friends think of me?" I asked myself impatiently.

A soft voice from somewhere inside seemed to answer, "Because you are caught in a trap. Your friendships are shallow and meaningless, and you are trying to fit into the mold they want you to fit. You can't live for them and for God at the same time. You must choose between them."

I didn't know where such absurd thoughts were coming from, nor did I have time to ponder them, for the curtain was about to rise.

I walked out on stage singing my lines, attempting to fall into the role of my character. Yet I was aware of a slight reserve in the back of my mind that kept me from fully devoting all I could to the performance. "After all," I reasoned, "I don't want to seem 'uncool' in front of my friends."

There were many congratulations and compliments after the play ended. As I came into the entrance of the sanctuary to find my parents, I was greeted by a tall, handsome young man with sparkling black eyes and dark curly hair.

"You did a wonderful job up there," he said warmly and extended his hand. "My name is Eric Ludy."

After we had exchanged pleasantries and engaged in a few minutes of small talk, Eric mentioned something which sparked my interest right away.

"I've just been talking with your mother and discovered you write music. I've just begun writing music myself, and I'd be interested in any help you could give me. Do you have some songs I could hear?"

I smiled and promised to bring my tape to church the next week for him to borrow. I was starting to ask him a question when I was interrupted by a church member offering a compliment on my performance in the play. I quickly said goodbye to the dark young stranger and for the next few days the incidence of our meeting did not come into my mind. Little did I know the significance of that short introduction. God was on the verge of turning my life upside down though I was completely unaware of the amazing adventures that lay just around the corner.

6

# *Maybe I Just Don't Belong Here*
## *Leslie*

My sixteenth birthday came and went. The wonderful romantic experience of being "sweet sixteen" that I'd always dreamed of had not happened. In fact, I was only growing more and more depressed.

The weeks passed, Christmas came, and before I knew it, a new year had begun. My normally cheerful countenance was now darkened by a sad expression. My vibrant, energetic personality had faded into a restless attitude. Even my most flippant friends noticed the change.

"What's wrong with you, Leslie?" they would question with mild frustration. "You're no fun anymore. You're always so serious. You need to loosen up!"

I knew I was far from "loosening up." Something was taking place inside my heart. Truth I had been attempting to deny for the past three years had finally come to stare me straight in the face, and now there was no denying it. I simply did not belong in this social frenzy.

For the first time since entering high school, I began to seriously examine the way I was living and the environment in which I was spending the majority of my time. True, my friends were all "Christians" and they were in youth groups at church; yet there was no difference between the way they were living and all my unbelieving peers. Lying, gossiping, back-stabbing, and perverted language were all things I had grown accustomed to hearing over the last few years. Now that I really analyzed the situation, I realized that I had been compromising by allowing all these things to creep into my life.

Also I began noticing the horrible cruelty of the dating scene. I watched helplessly as one friend after another "fell in love" with boys who only wanted to use them. Repeatedly my friends came away devastated and some even scarred for life. I had always been more careful; I had vowed never to give myself away physically to anyone until marriage. Yet I still came away from each temporary dating relationship with a bruised and hurting heart. As I struggled to comprehend why, I began to realize that most everyone involved in dating was motivated by selfish desires solely for the purpose of temporary security or pleasure.

For the first time my eyes were opened to how very wrong this behavior was. Why had I bought into this system of selfishness? I thought I was doing so well keeping to a commitment of abstinence until marriage (which was more than most of the kids were doing); yet I still felt deep wounds from all the temporary relationships I had been involved in. I had devoted my time and affections to various young men who really cared nothing about me! I had felt the sting of "breaking up" each time I passed an ex-boyfriend in the hall. Our eyes would meet, but we wouldn't acknowledge each other.

I knew I hadn't really *loved* any of the boys I dated. I had always seen these temporary relationships as being just for fun. If dating was so innocent, though, why did I feel a sharp pain in the pit of my stomach and my cheeks glow crimson each time I saw one of those young men that had vanished from my life as quickly as he entered my heart? Though I had not given myself to any of these young men physically, I still felt robbed and defiled, as if they had seen a part of me that was to be saved . . . my emotions.

"Why should I keep giving my heart away to one boy after another?" I asked myself.

The thought of living through another two and a half years of high school without being a part of the dating scene, however, seemed more than I could handle. But God was gently opening my eyes, and I began to feel very uncomfortable about becoming involved with anyone.

As I walked through the chaotic halls during passing period amidst a hurricane of conversation, laughter, and slamming lockers, for the first time I really saw the peers I had spent nearly every waking hour of my time with for the past three years. What were they living for anyway? The most important issues in their lives were which boy likes what girl, which friend is in a fight with whom, and how the football team played last Friday night.

I was stunned by the emptiness of it all and sickened by the realization that I had been completely wasting my life on such pettiness for so long. I knew there was more to being a teenager than this. Sure, being young could be fun, but to chase after empty and shallow ambitions throughout high school couldn't be right.

As much as I wanted to justify such feelings away, I was powerless to do so. I was determined that I would not waste my life on foolishness anymore, even if it meant losing all my friends and my popularity. I wanted to do something more with my life, but what? It wouldn't be long before I would find out.

# A Hidden Message from God
## Eric

Every February 2nd God and I share a little celebration together. You see, it was on a February 2nd that God really touched my life and my intimate relationship with Him began.

I grew up in a wonderful Christian home, and yet for some reason I always leaned more to the erroneous belief that God was in need of my life rather than that I was in desperate need of God. I misunderstood salvation to be more by merit of my family upbringing than a personal knowledge of Jesus Christ as my Lord and Savior.

It was on a February 2nd in 1990 that God sovereignly touched my life with a revelation of the tremendous cost He paid on account of my sins. He'd given His very life for me! I realized the least I could possibly give would be my life in return. Since that special day, February 2nd's have been loaded with endearing reminders from God of His love for me.

Well, it was now February 2nd, 1992, and all throughout the day I had expectantly awaited that something special that God was sure to do. After all, this was our anniversary!

A couple months had passed since the strange coincidence surrounding that smiling brunette had occurred. Quite frankly, it had faded from my mind. There I sat at the Runkles' dining room table deeply distracted from the conversation that buzzed around me. The day had come and gone, and it seemed God had forgotten our celebration day. I battled not to give into self-pity.

It was the first time our family had ever spent an evening with the Runkles, and I'm sure I made a fine guest as I fumbled with discouragement within. Still I molded a flimsy smile outwardly, trying to cover up my inner struggle. I burrowed through the night with all the intensity of a turtle.

As we prayed in the living room following dinner, I asked God to speak to me, to place a prayer within my heart, but no prayers of eloquence came. I opened my eyes amidst the prayer and caught a glimpse of a young brunette with her eyes closed as her head nodded in heavenly supplication. Scenes from two months earlier grew wings and fluttered to the foreground of my thoughts. Once again, the soft and delicate voice known by my heart spoke, "Eric, this is your wife."

Em' words were fightin' words! "I don't know who that devil thinks he is, but he's taken this way too far," I thought. "And in the middle of a prayer time?! How dare he attempt to distract me with such ridiculousness! This girl is but sixteen years old and younger than my kid brother by a good two years. How preposterous!"

I suppressed the invading thought with a violent rebuke and attempted to focus again upon my Lord. Now a bit shaken, I remained silent throughout the rest of the prayer asking God to clear my mind and keep my motives pure toward this young sister in the Lord. Still God did not speak to me. Listlessly I stuck my arms in my coat sleeves and prepared to walk out into the brisk night air after all the "thank you's" and "good-bye's" were offered.

"Eric," the mother of the young brunette called suddenly.

I turned to find her pleasant face determinedly perusing my demeanor with a tenderness and concern.

"I believe God would want you to know," she began with a serene countenance, "that what you heard from Him tonight was truly from Him."

My mind raced through my inventory of experiences acquired throughout the night and failed to find one that would hold such a regal status as to be titled, "Message from God." I charitably smiled in return, void of any response.

"Does that make sense to you?" she sweetly inquired.

"Well, I . . . I will pray about it," I fidgeted.

That February 2nd melted away at midnight, unable to offer any immediate blossom of celebration. Yet like a seed that is hidden for a time in the soil of obscurity, it would eventually grow to be a fragrant flower displaying God's amazing providence.

# Totally Surrendered to God
## Leslie

During the first few months of 1992 I spent some time with different members of the Ludy family. I always enjoyed being with them, perhaps because they were not in any way connected to my high school life. It was refreshing!

The two young men in the family, Eric and Mark, were unlike any boys I had ever known. They were twenty-one and eighteen and seemed to have none of the conceited attitudes or perverted mind-sets that all the high school boys I knew had. Eric and Mark appeared to have no interest in dating relationships but rather were totally consumed in their walks with the Lord. As a result, I felt no pressure when I was around them to act any certain way. I could simply be myself and was assured they would always treat me as a younger sister.

After our brief meeting at the Christmas play, Eric and I had spent a few afternoons working on music together. For years songwriting had been my special way of expressing the feelings and convictions in my heart. Not many of my friends even knew I wrote. Eric had found the same outlet of expression. I felt totally comfortable sharing my music with him. He in turn shared his songs with me. His songs overflowed with passion and deep emotion. It was obvious they came from a highly intimate fellowship between him and his Lord. I was both fascinated and inspired by this charismatic young Christian man. He seemed to be on the cutting edge of something I wanted so desperately—a more committed walk with the Lord and a deeper purpose to my life.

Though Eric never spoke about his experience in college, I had heard from others that he had been doing quite well there. He had been successful academically and had been well liked by his peers. There appeared to be no logical reason for him to have left. Then I heard that he had decided to leave because he felt God leading him to go into missions for a period of time. And I had heard something even more amazing about this fascinating young man. He had deliberately chosen not to date but to trust God to bring him his wife.

"Why," I wondered with great curiosity, "did he decide to leave college, give up his friends, and stop dating?"

As we drove home one evening through rush hour traffic after a voice lesson together, he told me the story of God's "getting a hold of his life."

"Coming home for Christmas break one year," he said, "I was in a major car accident. My roommate was going over fifty miles per hour in a blizzard. We suddenly hit black ice and went airborne over a hill, rolled, and landed at the bottom of the hill. The truck was totaled, but Bob and I were amazingly unhurt.

"When the police officer came and examined the accident, he pointed to me and said, 'You shouldn't be here right now. I don't know why you're still alive.'

"I knew God saved my life that day. The message He spoke to my heart was, 'Life is fragile; give yours to Me.'

"I realized that even though I had been calling myself a Christian and living by Christian morals, I had really been living for myself. I saw that I had made all kinds of plans for myself without consulting God. After that I determined that instead of

27

trying to fit God into my life, I was going to give my life completely to Him."

Not long after the accident, Eric began to rapidly grow in intimacy with the Lord. He felt God calling him out of pre-med into missions. People told him he was throwing his life away, wasting his talents. Yet he knew he had heard God's leading. Even though leaving college was one of the most difficult things he ever had to do, that radical step of obedience was a turning point for him in his Christian walk.

Eric's testimony had a great impact upon my young heart. I could see that he was a very gifted young man with the ability to accomplish anything he set his mind to; yet he was totally surrendered to God.

"That's the key 'being totally surrendered to God,'" I said to myself. I knew that was where I wanted my life to be; yet I still wasn't quite sure how to do it. I had prayed lots of times, confessing to God that He was Lord of my life, but I knew I wasn't really living on the cutting edge of a deep, daily walk with Him. It seemed impossible to grow in intimacy with Him when my whole life was consumed with an endless cycle of friends, boys, schoolwork, and parties.

How could I escape the trap I was in and become as Eric, on that cutting edge, not living for myself but for Him?

## Stripped of My Coolness
### ___ Leslie ___

Shortly after that memorable conversation in the car, I decided to take a week off from school and go to a mission base in Tyler, Texas with Eric and Mark and my brother, David. That week away from the phone and the daily routine of school became the turning point of my Christian life.

Alone in my hotel room, as I prayed about all that was taking place in my life, it became increasingly clear what I was to do. God was requiring me not only to give everything to Him in my heart, but then to live my commitment out through my life. He was asking me to take a radical step of obedience—one I wasn't quite sure I was ready to take. I knew that for me to follow Him completely I would have to leave high school and get out of such a corrupt and distracting environment. I was to finish my education at home!

"Leave high school?" I thought incredulously. "How can God ask me to leave high school? To make that decision will mean I will not only lose all my friends and destroy my reputation, but that I will spend the rest of my teenage years doing nothing but staring out the window, lonely and depressed."

No fate seemed worse than leaving high school and becoming what I had termed a "dork". . . a home-schooler. Still no matter how much my mind protested, my heart knew it was God's will for me.

I arrived home from that trip to Texas on a Friday night and told my parents that God had spoken to me that I was not to go back to high school. They were shocked, to say the least, but after praying about it, they also felt it was right.

I never went back to high school. My friends heard through the grapevine what I had decided to do. Instantly almost all of them vanished from my life as if they had never existed. They were ready to forget me if I wasn't going to be one of them anymore. This didn't surprise me; it only made me all the more aware of just how shallow most of my friendships had been.

Ever since the day I left high school I have never been the same. That one step of obedience seemed to open up endless adventures with the Lord that I never knew existed until I finally ventured out of my comfort zone.

My initial mind-set that leaving high school would destine me to a life of apathetic isolation was completely destroyed within the first few weeks of being home. I found I had no time to be lonely or bored for God was busy at work in my heart. He was cleansing me of all the "junk" I had allowed into my life from being in public school and replacing the worldly ways that had been indoctrinated into my mind with His perfect ways.

# *Waiting vs. Dating*
## *Leslie*

One of the first areas to be dealt with in my heart was dating.

In high school dating had been all fun and games for me. I thought I was doing what was normal—dating casually for a few years, then when I was old enough to seriously consider marriage, I would meet the right man and fall in love with him. God now showed me how very wrong such a mind-set had been.

I saw that I had been involved in the dating scene for purely selfish reasons, without at all considering my future husband or my boyfriends' future wives. By flirting and spending time with boys, and thus drawing their attention and affections to me, I was actually stealing what belonged to their future wives. By giving my emotions away to one boy after another, I was giving away something meant only for my husband. I had upheld a commitment to abstinence, but I had not understood true purity.

I began to see that true purity was rooted in the heart; it meant that every thought, attitude, or emotion I allowed in must be honoring to my future husband and pleasing to God.

From then on I determined to abandon all dating relationships and to trust that God, in His perfect timing, would bring
my husband to me. In the meantime, I made a commitment to
my future husband that I would seek to do him "good and not
evil all the days of my life," as the Proverbs 31 woman had
done.

Of course, I did not make this commitment without hes-
itation. There were many doubts that entered my mind. "What
if God doesn't really bring him to me? Or worse yet, what if
God brings someone I'm not at all attracted to?" The only
answer I had to counter these foreboding questions was a quiet
inner peace which simply said, "Trust Me."

I asked God to help me take my mind off relationships with
the opposite sex and to "fall asleep" in Him—to become so
consumed in my relationship with Him that I would never even
miss the dating relationships I had given up. He did just that.
Over the next few months, many godly young men came into my
life. For the first time ever I was able to have pure friendships
with boys, undefiled by ulterior motives. I was free from
worrying about whether they "liked" me or not; they were
simply older brothers to me.

My friendship with Eric continued to deepen. He was
always a tremendous encouragement to me in my walk with the
Lord. God seemed to have granted us a special spiritual kindred-
ness, and we were able to write songs and minister together.

The majority of the time we spent with each other was with
our two families when we were fellowshipping together. In this
relaxed and real environment, our families were able to see our
friendship grow based on a foundation of purity.

By this time we both had developed strong convictions about
relationships with the opposite sex, and we were very careful to
see that even our boy/girl friendships were of the utmost purity.
We seemed to have an unspoken agreement that, no matter how
much we enjoyed each other's company, we would not cross a
certain threshold in which our emotions could leak out in any

way and thus destroy our friendship with each other and dishonor our future mates.

I can honestly say that though I loved to be with Eric and deeply cherished the fellowship we had, I did not consider our relationship one that would ever exceed friendship. He was five years older than I, and I considered him an older brother.

## Malarkey from Marky
### Eric

I used to think, "She's out there somewhere. I wonder if she's thinking about me?" I would write letters to her, even songs, and every night I purposed to lift her up before the Throne of Grace and ask Christ to work in her life molding her into His likeness.

Constantly I was goaded with the challenging thought that if I desired my future wife to remain innocent and pure for me, how much more would she desire my innocence and purity to be saved for her. After a lifetime of not living that way, I determined to live as if she were watching my life and to question myself, "If my future bride could see me right now, would she feel comfortable with how I'm interacting with this young lady?"

Months had passed, and my brother and I had grown to be close friends with Leslie. I had known many Christian girls but few, very few, who shared an excitement and passion for the things of God as did this smiling brunette. I was intrigued by this young lady and often had thoughts of how she would one day make quite a wife for my younger brother or possibly for my good friend, David, who I knew also loved the Lord. I wanted the very best for her, and I knew that either Marky, (a fond name for my younger brother), or David would make a terrific husband.

I felt responsible, before God, to be an example of a godly man for her life. When Marky told me that he thought I was going to marry Leslie, my livid, defensive, and utterly sincere response was, "No! I think *you* are going to marry Leslie!" For months I had battled with keeping my thoughts and motives absolutely pure toward this young girl, and I sure wasn't going to accept any malarkey from my little brother.

# *Mysterious Tears*
## *Eric*

Leslie and her mother, Janet, had joined our family on a week long missions project in inner-city New Orleans. The week went well, and we seemed to make it through the balmy heat with smiles and a song still in our hearts. But something was nagging me . . . my relationship with this innocent young girl.

We were spending quite a bit of time together working on music, taking voice lessons, attending the same church, and even studying history together. I was really beginning to think that maybe we were spending too much time with one another. If my wife were to come into my life right now, how would she feel about the large amount of time I was spending with this young girl? Even more importantly, if Leslie's future husband were to come into her life right now, would he feel comfortable about how much time she was spending with me?

My mind was perplexed with how I should deal with this, and I bludgeoned myself with accusation. How could I be so insensitive as to devote so much time to a sixteen-year-old girl?

As we drove home from New Orleans in a rented mini-van, I knew it was time to address this issue. Everyone else had fallen asleep in the back. The moment was ripe as I drove and Leslie sat beside me in the front seat.

"Leslie?" I muttered sheepishly.

Her eyes turned to inquire and her soft voice offered a pleasant, "Yes?"

"Uh . . . ," I didn't know how to say it. How could I possibly express to this delicate young girl that I felt maybe we shouldn't spend as much time together? "Uh . . . ," I continued. I offered up a quick prayer, beckoning God's help, realizing that if He was the One placing this on my heart, He would also give me a way of expressing it to Leslie.

I felt like I started with thunder, and I just knew this would bruise her tender heart. Yet as I continued, it seemed to turn to a soft, ministering rain. I realized that she, too, shared my concern. We both wanted to be so careful in all our relations outside of the marriage relationship, and she seemed to be even touched by the fact I was considering her relationship with her future husband. In the end, we decided we would spend a week seeking guidance regarding our friendship.

As we talked, two amazing things took place. Both of us later could only admire these two things as God's handiwork leading us in His perfect way.

There was a tape playing in the mini-van, offering a dramatic background to our discussion. It was unfamiliar to me, and I really didn't even give thought to the fact that it was playing. Right in the middle of our discussion there was a song change, and as it began, I just suddenly started to weep.

Tears streamed down my face as Leslie just sat there and wondered what she might have spoken that would have touched me in such a profound way. Neither of us spoke, and both sets of ears attuned themselves to the song that accompanied these mysterious tears welling in my eyes and dripping down my cheeks.

The song was entitled "How Beautiful." It was all about Christ's radiant bride. I was very aware of how strange this was, and I pleaded with God not to let Leslie think what I was thinking. She knew very well that I didn't cry easily. The song ended and so did the tears. Neither of us discussed it; we simply carried on as if it had never happened.

It wasn't long after that strange incident that I spoke something to my lovely friend that I wished at the time hadn't slipped out of my mouth. I didn't even know why I said it.

"I think I should talk with your father," I blundered, desiring to stuff those words back into my mouth like a messy burrito.

Before I could make any more verbal fauxpas, she excitedly responded, "I think you should, too!"

Later, I discovered that she had also felt terribly awkward after her hasty agreement, not really understanding why she felt it was such a good idea either. Whether we knew it or not, it was God's idea, and "Weird Week" had officially begun.

# Weird Week
## Eric

Names are like glue. After a certain amount of time they can't be removed. To Leslie's dismay, the name to this day remains, "Weird Week"—the week God began to do some really weird things.

It was a week spent seeking correction, but for some reason I never felt the sharp sting of a loving reprimand from my heavenly Father.

Friday came, the day of Leslie's and my voice lesson. We hadn't seen each other throughout the week, and it was fun to be together again. I didn't have any big revelations from God—any great words of wisdom about how we should handle our relationship—so I sort of shied away from that line of discussion.

I was singing for a wedding that Saturday, and the rehearsal was that night. After voice lessons, we both decided it would be easier just to have Leslie come along with me to the rehearsal instead of my taking her all the way back home.

We sat upon a pew in a sparsely filled wedding chapel awaiting my turn to get up and do a microphone check. A young lady was called up before me and asked to sing her song. Leslie and I sat awkwardly staring about, taking in the quaint beauty of this tiny wedding chapel.

As the young lady's music began, my heart dropped, my tongue went dry, and tingles went up my spine. I stared forward and prayed, "Don't let Leslie think what I just thought. Here we are in a wedding chapel, the week we determined to set aside to pray about our relationship, and this girl, who knows absolutely nothing about our situation, is singing the very song I mysteriously wept to in the mini-van on our way home from New Orleans!"

"How Beautiful" played and my heart palpitated. It was surely not discussed between us, just forever embedded in the soil of our memories.

# The Bride in the Mirror
## Leslie

To me "Weird Week," as Eric so eloquently termed it, was more than just weird. It was downright shocking!

Throughout the week, as I prayed about my friendship with Eric and sought correction and guidance, several unusual events took place. Though I was asking God to show me how to pull away from our friendship in order to keep myself set apart for my husband, the only response I received in return was the awareness, "This relationship is of Me. It is good. I have placed you and Eric together for a special purpose."

None of this made sense to me. Were these just my emotions, speaking to my mind to deceive me? Had I given part of my heart to this young man and, therefore, was unable to hear God's voice in the matter? I just couldn't figure out what the Lord was trying to say to me, so I continued to pray.

Toward the end of that week, I was listening to a Twila Paris tape and cleaning my room. When the song, "How Beautiful," came on, it captured my attention. It was speaking of Christ's radiant bride. This was the song Eric had mysteriously wept through on our way home from New Orleans. What could it mean?

As I turned to walk across the room, I caught my reflection in the large mirror overhanging my dresser. My red sweatshirt and blue jeans faded into a beautiful white wedding dress. I saw myself as a bride, with tears of joy glistening in my eyes. I was radiant with happiness, for on this day my destiny was to be fulfilled—to be placed at the side of the man I had been created to serve. It made me catch my breath. Never before had I envisioned so clearly what marriage was all about.

The song eventually ended along with my daydreams. Was God trying to speak to me through this? I didn't often think of marriage for I felt it would be many years before God would reveal my husband to me. Now during this "Weird Week" while I was praying about my friendship with Eric, why couldn't I get the subject of marriage off my mind?

*15*

# Gulp!!
## Eric

With sweaty palms and a swarm of butterflies awakened in the pit of my stomach, I met with Rich Runkles, Leslie's father, adding an appropriate finishing touch to a truly "Weird Week." I'm sure smoke was probably rising from my ears as I deliberated what I should say to this man. Here I was, barging into his busy schedule, and I really wasn't even sure why. My tongue was a little weightier in my mouth, and my lips were strangely zapped of all moisture and peculiarly sticky. I felt as if this man of God was reading me like a newspaper, and I was one of those comic strips that attempts to be humorous but miserably bombs.

Throughout the week I had sought God's correction. I just knew I would finally be waylaid with a necessary dose of conviction. I had it coming. I had insensitively built a friendship with a girl five years younger than I. In the process I had spent far too much time with her. I awaited the blustery winds of reprimand as Rich calmly pondered all the questions and honest concerns in my youthful heart. Then lightning struck.

"Eric," came his grave reply, "do you know how I know your relationship with my daughter is pure?"

My mind scrambled to gain a hold and offer my face at least a serene smile, but I remained petrified in light of the possible point he was making. He then continued with the golden phrase I'll surely never forget as long as I live: "Because if it wasn't, God would tell me."

My heart dropped, and I froze in the state of contemplation. I was struck with the revelation of the God-given authority a father has over the life of his daughter. I trembled to think of invading it, or even treating it as if it were not there. Leslie was his treasure. It was his sacred duty to protect and provide for her well being. Right at the point where he should be telling me to bug off, I found him encouraging our friendship instead of correcting it.

"Eric," he began again, "do you know how I know your friendship with Leslie is from God? Because ever since you've been friends, I've seen her only grow closer to Jesus."

The expected fiery showers of discipline surprisingly never came. He taught me of his daughter instead of lecturing me on how far I should stay away from her. As we talked, I saw how very much he understood his daughter and how very much he loved her. I began to understand that there was a bubble of protection about Leslie that neither I nor any other man should ever dare invade. During that memorable afternoon, I realized that there was a proper entrance into this young girl's life, and it was found in the man that I trembled before as I ate my lunch.

Rich seemed to know more than he was letting on, but he was content to let me search for answers instead of just handing them to me on a silver platter. He seemed to understand my concerns and encouraged me to continue to seek God's highest. But he added a very strange twist, making me wonder whether he had understood a word I had just spoken.

"Eric, I give you my blessing to pursue a relationship with my daughter in any way that God leads you."

There was an awkward pause as my mind tried to digest the words just spoken. Didn't he know I was not interested in furthering a relationship with his daughter? I thought it must have been obvious that Leslie and I were a good five years apart in age, and there was something horribly wrong in that . . . wasn't there?

Rich's blessing turned out to be much more significant than I knew at the time. Soon I would appreciate what God had providentially accomplished in this "Weird Week."

# On the Edge of the Threshold
## Leslie

I cannot tell you the exact day or hour when the thought first came into my mind. It seemed to be something I had always known, yet never understood, and it crept up upon me unawares like a long-lost childhood memory suddenly recalled. "Eric is your future husband."

I hardly dared entertain such bold speculations; yet I couldn't seem to hold myself back from believing it. I knew Eric had been getting together with my father, but that was simply for counsel on our friendship and perhaps other issues Eric happened to be dealing with. What was so unusual about his meeting with my dad? I tried to reason with myself not to blow the situation out of proportion, but the events of the next few weeks only served to increase my perplexing anxieties.

"Dad?" I ventured one day after my father returned home from a meeting with Eric. "What did you and Eric talk about today?"

"If Eric wants you to know, he'll tell you himself," was the elusive but not unkind reply. His answer only heightened my wonder and curiosity. The more I had prayed about it, the more certain I became that God was showing me my husband-to-be in Eric. Yet Eric had said nothing to indicate that he felt a similar leading. What if I were to give my emotions to him and later find out that he wasn't the one I was to spend my life with?

I certainly was not about to bring the subject up to Eric. I did not care to make a fool of myself by taking the initiative that was rightfully his, but even more importantly, I was ever careful of the threshold I had vowed never to cross. I knew that for Eric and I to even discuss the possibility of a relationship beyond what we already had would be passing the point of no return. We would then destine ourselves to two options—to get married, or to exchange our pure friendship for one strained by awkwardness. Since I valued our friendship so highly, it terrified me to think of destroying it by one foolish mistake.

# I Know!!
### Eric

I know!" I shockingly told myself. "I know!" Why I suddenly "knew" I had absolutely no idea. But I knew! There I sat at my desk and in a matter of moments, like a veil lifted from my eyes, I could suddenly see God's obvious fingerprints all over Leslie's and my relationship. One second I was blind, and in the next I could perfectly see. "I know!" I repeated with solemn wonder. "I know!"

Why I couldn't see it during the many months preceding I didn't have a clue, except for the fact that during that time God had enabled us to build a true friendship.

Mothers seem to have those intuitive hunches about things like romance. Right in line with her calling, my mother had attempted to express to me how she felt Leslie and I were meant for one another. At the time I was still extremely defensive toward that line of thinking and bombastically responded, "If God wants me to marry Leslie Runkles, He's going to have to send an angel down from heaven to make that clear."

How I had gone from a brazen statement like that to knowing Leslie would someday be my bride, I can only attribute to the sovereign grace of God. I wasn't visited by an angel, but it seems I was visited by something far greater. God seemed to illuminate the past few years of my life, allowing me to see His tender hand of providential care. From giving up this area of my life in the first place, to coming back to Colorado to study voice, to the mental snapshot of this beautiful unknown brunette as I prayed for my wife, to the Christmas play, to that discouraging February 2nd, all the way to the strange meeting with Rich as we arrived back from New Orleans, God had been so gently working in my life in such a way that I could always be certain it was His perfect work in bringing Leslie and me together.

Our ages had always been such an issue, but now it seemed to just fade away. I had begun to realize, in a profound way, why God had led me to speak with Rich. This tremendous treasure of Leslie, so delicate and beautiful, was entrusted to him. It was his responsibility to protect this treasure and provide for her spiritual, emotional, and physical needs. He held the keys of spiritual authority over her life, and God was showing me how sacred this bubble that protected her truly was. If God was going to bless our relationship, then I must enter this bubble through the proper door . . . through the blessing of her father.

# Gulp Again!!
## Eric

The moment I had anticipated throughout my entire life, with a mixture of both excitement and dread, had finally come. I didn't practice in front of the mirror or rehearse my lines like all the young men in the black and white movies I'd seen. Rich awaited me at Perkins' Family Restaurant. If you want to get time with Rich, you pretty much have to be willing to meet with him in the early morning hours before he heads off to work. So there we were before the crack of dawn. Boy, would he be surprised what would accompany his bacon and eggs this early morning! His eyes drooped as he sipped his coffee while trying his hardest to listen to what I had to say.

"Rich," I squeaked, as I gulped and tried to speak at the same time. "I believe God has shown me that Leslie is, one day, to be my wife."

It was pure adrenalin that carried me through. Since God had shown me that Leslie was the one, I'd been like a man on a mission to do this whole thing right. I felt the wisest thing I could do was to submit this before Rich and pray about it with him. Maybe he would feel differently, but I was gambling that he felt the very same.

It was amazing what a rejuvenating effect this one simple statement had upon Rich's drooping eyelids. After a few moments, when he had regulated his heartbeat once again, he said, "You know, Eric, Janet and I have been praying for Leslie's husband for fourteen years, asking God that we would recognize him when he finally came along. We both have felt for quite awhile that you are that one."

Any young man who has ventured to propose to a father such a notion about the probability of marrying his daughter surely can appreciate the relief and thrill that came as he said those words.

Rich was a man I deeply respected, but I really had no entrance point into his busy life of work and ministry. Well, on that early morning shared with the Perkins' waitress, I found the silver key. You start dealing with Rich's daughter, and you start dealing with Rich's heartstrings. It truly was God's divine wisdom to win Leslie's heart by first going through the man that knew her better than any man alive. At first I was quite intimidated with the thought of talking about things so dear and intimate to my heart with a man I hardly knew. But as we continued to meet, our friendship grew and deepened. Over time, I discovered one of my very best friends in Leslie's father.

*19*

# Prayers and Pepperoni
## Eric

For months Leslie and I had shared a relationship marked by simple friendship and joy in the fact that we were both lovers of Christ. Now something different was taking place between us. Suddenly looking at each other in the eyes was becoming difficult because our eyes gave away the stirrings within our hearts. Our times together became almost awkward as we both sensed the pull to express a deeper longing for a life shared together . . . but we didn't speak a word.

Weeks had passed since I had spoken with Rich about Leslie's one day being my bride, but I was waiting for God to move me forward in sharing with Leslie. I knew those words would alter our relationship forever. I had known how to be a good friend, an older brother who would always stand up and defend her, but I sure didn't know the first thing about how to take it any further than that. I could sense Leslie crying out from behind her stoic demeanor that she needed to hear some verbal expression of commitment to her life. Very hesitant to do anything rash, I asked my father and Rich if the three of us could get together over pizza and talk.

The pizza was superb, but the night will be remembered long after for the prayers and not for the pepperoni. That night we all agreed that it was time for me to share with Leslie. We felt God had opened up for us a time to prepare for our eventual engagement. None of us had ever heard of any such thing before, but we felt this was God's leading.

Both fathers placed their hands on me and blessed the newly budding relationship. The prayers were beautiful and seemed to be in the most perfect order. It was simply incredible to be in such perfect unity with the two men who held the spiritual authority in both Leslie's and my life. It was as if God was smiling and saying, "This is right!"

The words that crescendoed in my heart that night were spoken by Rich. "Eric, tonight I give you my blessing to win my daughter's heart for marriage."

I didn't know why God had put a lock over my mouth for so many weeks and I hadn't spoken anything to Leslie, yet I would never doubt thereafter that it was God's wisdom holding me back until I heard those words. With those words from Rich seemed also to come the very blessing of God. It was now time for me to cross the threshold into a relationship with Leslie.

2.0

# *The Grassy Hill*
## *Leslie*

W eeks passed, and still nothing had happened. Eric and I continued getting together often to work on music or study history, yet I knew something was being left undiscussed between us. Was God speaking anything to him about our relationship?

I had no idea what he and my dad had been discussing or how he felt the Lord leading in regard to our friendship and it frustrated me. I came to the point in my own emotions where I felt I simply wanted to know. Was Eric to be my future husband or not? If not, I knew I must back away from seeing him so much for my emotions were beginning to be stirred.

Finally one day it happened. Eric came to my house and asked if I wanted to take a walk. He said he had talked with both of our fathers the night before and now wanted to discuss something with me.

"At last!" I said to myself with relief. "Maybe this will help clarify what has been going on inside me lately."

As we sat side by side on a grassy hill under the warm August sun, Eric spoke the words of significance I had been needing to hear for so many weeks.

The conversation on that grassy hill did wonders to calm my anxious thoughts. As Eric is famous for doing, he began his speech with a ten-minute soliloquy to dramatize the point. Once he got to the meat of it, however, I realized that God had been showing him over the last few weeks that I was the one he was to marry. Not only that, he had been meeting with my father to discuss all God was speaking to him, and both my parents also felt that one day Eric and I were to be married. This gave me great security and confirmed that all the strange things I had felt God showing me since "Weird Week" were really from Him.

# One Big Happy Family
## Leslie

Just a few days after our talk on the grassy hill, Eric and I united with every member from each of our families and had a time of praise and rejoicing in what God had done. We marveled at God's faithfulness as each member of both families took turns sharing the different ways in which God had shown them personally that our relationship was of Him. It seemed to be a sacred bond between our two families. By the end of the evening, we knew that we had all become "one big family" because of the beautiful work God had done between us.

We all agreed to keep this new relationship God had given Eric and me just between our two families for a time because of its sacredness and because of how new and different it all was. It proved to be a very wise decision. It was a special tie shared between the ten of us for over a year and brought us closer together than anything else ever could have.

2 2

# Preparation for Engagement
## _____ Leslie _____

Eric and I knew that it would be a long while before either of us were ready for marriage. I was still in my last year of high school, and I had so much yet to learn before I would be able to face the task of running a home. Eric was still seeking direction for his future in the areas of his calling, education, and finances. He was planning to leave in a few months for another year at missionary school.

My dad had been teaching Eric and me about the three stages of unity in a relationship: spiritual, emotional, then after marriage, physical. We were now in a time of working on our spiritual unity which still needed to deepen and grow. He counseled us that emotional unity should come only after engagement, and that our engagement should be short because emotions are designed to lead to physical oneness which was only to take place in marriage.

Eric and I agreed that we were in a season of "preparation for engagement" when God would begin to deepen the spiritual oneness between us. We knew that we needed to be very careful not to awaken emotions before it was time since it would be a while before engagement was reasonable or timely. Because of this, we purposed to give our emotions to God. We knew that only He could hold them in check. We could never do it in our own strength, but by His grace, we would be able to continue in a friendship based in purity despite the new revelation of our future marriage.

Giving our emotions for each other to God was one of the wisest things we ever did in our relationship. We were free to grow in our individual walks with the Lord without being distracted by overwhelming feelings for each other.

We decided it also would be wise, as a testimony of giving our emotions to God, to withhold physical affection from each other—even simple things such as hugging or kissing. I must admit that if someone had told me a year earlier that I would not kiss my husband until our wedding day, I would have burst out laughing. I had never heard of something so extreme or unrealistic. Yet now, with God in charge of every area of our relationship, it wasn't hard at all to make this commitment. With God controlling our emotions for one another, we were able to go on in a deeper friendship, maintaining the utmost purity. We knew that our physical relationship after marriage would be all the more beautiful as a result.

Eric left for a year away at missionary school. I stayed home and finished my high school education, focusing on my relationship with God and with my family. During this time Eric and I wrote letters to each other about the different ways we were growing closer to the Lord. This brought us closer together than we ever could have been had we not been separated.

After Eric returned from mission school, an opportunity arose for him to teach history and literature to a community of home-school children in another state not at all close to where I was living. Although I knew it meant we would be separated yet another year, I felt peaceful letting him go knowing God would bring us together in His perfect time. The fact that my emotions were given to the Lord and held in check by Him made it possible for me to do this so easily.

I continued to grow in friendship with different members of his family, as did my parents and two brothers. It was a special time of innocence and excitement. When Eric would come home to visit during vacations, our families would join together for many joyful and fun-filled reunions. Having our one big family surrounding Eric and me in love and fellowship brought both stability and life to our relationship.

# She's No Beefy Linebacker
## Eric

I had known how to be a friend, but I was quite intimidated by the thought of trying to win a young girl's heart for marriage. I knew the strategy of how to win at athletic competition, but this was a whole new ball game! This involved a delicate, fragile young lady—not a beefy linebacker who can take a few hits and never feel a thing.

My mother had always admonished me never to tell a girl I loved her unless I planned on marrying her. "Eric, as a man, you just don't understand what words can do to a woman," she would counsel me as only a loving mother could.

I yearned to do this God's way. So to my knees I went, bidding God to grant me heavenly wisdom and to show me how to move forward. I knew only too well how many times I'd blown it in relationships before. Then it had always been my way; now I longed for it to be God's way.

As I shared with Leslie all God had done, describing for her all the amazing fingerprints God had placed upon our lives together, I found myself being very discreet about my emotions for her. I found her to be an absolutely beautiful young woman, but I was hesitant to speak very much for I remembered that my mother had told me that Leslie would place a great deal of stock in the words I spoke to her. I chose to save certain words for special occasions—to say them in a way that she would always know I saved those words for her.

I felt that God had given me a treasure of purity when I was born. This treasure of purity was a gift that I could one day offer to my wife on our marriage day. It would forever be a symbol of my loyalty and devotion to her. She would be certain that if I could keep it polished and beautiful for her in the years prior to marriage, that certainly I would always keep it shined and shimmering throughout our life together.

I hadn't been the wisest steward of this treasure of purity in my high school years, and there was very little left of it by the time I realized how valuable it was and how important it was to keep sacred for my wife-to-be. There were many tears shed grieving over some of the decisions I had made growing up that I wished so badly I could somehow erase from my history. By God's grace I had remained a virgin physically, but mentally and emotionally I had given myself away many times.

I painfully shared with Leslie all the times I had offered her rightful treasure over to some other girl who now was just a haunting memory. My thought was that this would cause Leslie to distrust me and draw away. Rather, it worked to draw us closer and seemed to stir in Leslie a greater respect for my commitment to purity that I now held.

By God's design He took us far away from each other while the cement was still hardening in our infantile relationship. I headed off to a missionary school in Texas. What seemed to be incongruent with what God was doing between us turned out to be a solidifying factor in our relationship. We learned to express our hearts to one another through letters. It was definitely easier to keep the physical aspect of our relationship under wraps when we were a good thousand miles apart and to focus on the foundation stones of lifelong friendship.

Our families had agreed that this was to be a secret between us until God led otherwise. It was sometimes hard not to talk about all that God was doing with those I grew close to in Texas, but I found this secret bloom all the more beautiful in my heart as I treasured it like a precious bouquet from heaven.

Two years would pass with me somewhere far away. After Texas I headed up to Michigan to teach, only increasing the miles separating us. The times spent with one another were like candy that we savored and enjoyed with everything in us until I again would have to leave. Every time I saw Leslie she grew to be more beautiful, and every time I left I appreciated all the more the priceless jewel God had set aside for my life.

As those two years passed, an uneasiness began to grow within me about the thought of being away from Leslie for another year. Leslie, our parents, and I had all felt that God would make it clear when the time was ripe for me to propose. We didn't know quite how God would make that clear, but we felt that all of us would somehow just know that it was the right time to move forward another step.

For spring break in 1994 I headed back to Colorado. Leslie and I had felt it was time to share our relationship with the body of Christ back in our hometown. After we shared, it seemed a well of emotion was mysteriously unlocked between us. Now, more than ever, we felt the overwhelming river of love course through our hearts. God had held our emotions for so long, and He, for some reason, had deemed this as the proper time to unleash them.

I was supposed to leave the next morning for Michigan, but I didn't think I could possibly leave this young woman I loved so dearly. I remember sobbing in the car as I traveled up I-76 towards Nebraska. It seemed unjust for God to release something so very beautiful and then to pull us away from one another once again.

24

# The Little Mermaid Picture That Wasn't
## Eric

I couldn't help but wonder if the time was near. A great expectancy filled my heart and seemed to soothe the ache inside to be close to Leslie for I knew that possibly it was nearing the time for engagement.

My sister and I were in Michigan teaching together. We shared a trailer out in the country. Every night we prayed for Leslie's and my relationship and that I would have God's wisdom to know when to move forward.

There was one thing that my sister and I shared that no one else knew, including Leslie. We were agreeing in prayer every night that God would supernaturally provide the engagement ring. I desired to have a ring to present to Leslie when I proposed, but I sure didn't have the means financially to purchase something like that. So Krissy and I determined to ask God to miraculously provide this symbol of commitment.

As I had driven home to Michigan over the weekend, I had been unable to escape the ponderous notion, "Lord, is the time drawing near?" I asked God to show me in His own special way when it was time. He was now ready to make it very clear to my heart.

Early that following Monday morning I was in the bathroom getting ready for work. A tremendous expectancy bubbled within me like champagne itching to explode as the cork is loosened. I didn't know if I should sing or if I should shout, but I felt I needed to do something. Krissy was in the adjoining room spending time with Jesus.

"Krissy!" I shouted with a fervor that I'm sure startled her. A faint "yes" came through the wall boards. Her response did not match the excitement that gripped me.

"Krissy! Krissy! Come in here!" I hollered.

There was a shifting in the other room and then the sound of a door creeping open. "What is it, Eric?" She looked concerned.

I explained to her my great joy and tremendous expectancy. She graciously thanked me for sharing that with her and proceeded back to her time with her Lord which had been so rudely interrupted.

With a little kick in my step, I skipped about in the bathroom. I gave my hair an extra fluff with my comb and my teeth an added "voila" with my toothbrush as if I were accompanied by music. In the drama of the moment, I sifted about for my lotion but couldn't find it. Then I remembered I had forgotten to remove it from my coat pocket after I returned from the trip.

My coat was out in the front room, so I ventured out to retrieve my lotion. I dug in my coat pocket for the small white tube but found only an envelope. On the outside was written, "For Eric Ludy." I thought it must be another present from one of those cute little kids I worked with. They were always drawing little scribbles or coloring in "Little Mermaid" pictures and giving them to me.

I grinned as I searched the other pocket. I found the lotion and headed back to the bathroom, drinking in the beauty of life as if it were a tall glass of ice water on a hot summer day.

In the bathroom again, my curiosity got the better of me. I burrowed into this newly discovered gift to find out which precious child had been so thoughtful. My eyebrows raised and my heart pounded as I pulled out, not a scribbled work of art, but a huge wad of green papers with "In God We Trust" printed upon them.

"Krissy!" I hollered with urgency.

Her door burst open once again to come to my aid only to find me staring at her with a strange look on my face of horror and thrill with a dash of anxious wonder.

"What is it?" she courageously asked.

All I could do was point. I hadn't counted it; I'd just set it carefully down on the counter as if it was radioactive. Krissy picked it up, with her mouth gaping open, and counted it out loud. Both of us just stared at each other in the mirror.

"What do you think it's for?"

"I don't have any idea!" I said as I quickly figured out how much the tithe would be.

"Wait!" she exclaimed. "There's something written on this piece of paper."

There had been a piece of notebook paper wrapped about the money. On it there was an amazing hint.

"It says, 'He is Jehovah Jireh . . .' And look! There's a picture of a . . ." Her voice faltered. Then quietly and dramatically she added, "a ring!"

Almost two years had passed since I had talked with Rich about marrying his daughter. Was this God's way of showing me that it was now time? Speaking with my parents and with Leslie's parents confirmed that, sure enough, it was time.

Leslie grew up always dreaming about her wedding day, wondering what her dress would look like and how she would wear her hair. I grew up imagining how I would propose to my love and how I would sweep her off her feet like an awaited knight in shining armor. I had many romantic ideas growing up but none that would truly express to Leslie how much I delighted in her. I wanted my bride to think she was the most loved woman in the entire world. I didn't know how I would do it, but one thing I did know . . . it had to be the ultimate surprise.

THE STORY OF OUR COURTSHIP

# *Delight Thyself in the Lord*
## *Leslie*

Over two years had passed since my monumental decision to leave high school, but it seemed more like ten. God had transformed me so much and done such amazing things in my life since then that I hardly remembered life as it had been.

"Delight thyself also in the Lord, and He shall give thee the desires of thine heart" (Psalm 37:4 KJV).

"How very true!" I mused while reading through the Psalms in a quiet time one morning. This lovely verse caused me to reflect upon all that had happened in my life during the last few years.

As I recalled the loneliness and isolation I had expected to experience as a result of giving my teenage years to God, I couldn't help but laugh. What God had done since I made the decision to give every area of my life to Him had far surpassed all my former ideals of sweet sixteen romances and the senior prom. He had restored my innocence and showed me what He had created my youth to be—a time of discovery, of learning His ways and enjoying life in true purity of heart, and of preparation for what He had destined me to become. I knew that through giving my life to Him, all my dreams had come true in an even more beautiful way than I ever could have imagined. Not only that, I was confident that they would continue to come true as long as my delight was found always in my Lord.

As the days of our courtship swiftly passed, I couldn't help but stand in awe of the incredible gift God had given me in Eric.

I remembered my long forgotten fears that when God brought my husband to me I would have no attraction to him. Now, in hindsight, I wondered how I could ever have set my expectations of God so low. Eric was much more than I had ever desired in a husband. Not only was I attracted to him physically, but more importantly, I was drawn to his heart for God. He was a man of integrity and honor, and his purpose in our relationship was to lead me ever closer to Jesus. I could sense the amazing call God had upon his life, and I felt honored to be chosen as the one who would stand by his side.

"God," I exclaimed in amazement, "if this is how You've chosen to bless me, then You must care more about this area of my life than even I do!"

Through just *one* step of obedience, God had shown me what beautiful gifts He desires to bestow upon His children, if only we will trust Him.

# Expectancy
## Leslie

As the weeks and months of my eighteenth year passed, I began to see marriage looming closer upon the horizon. My friendship with Eric had been a wonderful time, but we were both sensing it would soon be time to move on to the next step . . . engagement.

Eric was still in Michigan teaching history and literature. It was April. I knew I would not see him until the school year ended, but secretly I entertained the hope that maybe over the summer Eric would feel God's leading that it was finally time to become engaged. I was beginning to feel restless. What was ahead? If it wasn't marriage, it most likely meant college or mission school, neither of which sounded especially inviting.

As I sat on my bed one evening enjoying the warm spring breeze from my open window and drinking in the brilliance of the sunset over the Rocky Mountains, I was strangely filled with a sudden burst of joy and anticipation. The feeling stayed with me throughout the night and over the next few days. I couldn't help but wonder if it meant God was about to do something incredible in my life. But what? It couldn't have to do with my relationship with Eric for he was over twelve hundred miles away. I wouldn't see him for at least another two months. What else could it be?

My life seemed to be at a standstill. I was still involved in music, but it wasn't the same without having Eric to sing with. I had recently felt led to pursue a medical education, perhaps nursing, but I was still uncertain of the timing for that endeavor. Besides, it just didn't interest me very much right now.

Over the next few days, I continued to pray that God would begin to unfold things for me. Little did I know that drastic changes were just around the corner.

## The Ultimate Surprise
### _____ Leslie _____

God invented romance." When I first heard this paradoxical statement, I thought it sounded sacrilegious. I had never paired God and romance together . . . until now. My ideas of true romance were being completely transformed. I had long since abandoned what I had been taught about the world's foolish and empty ideas of romance. Now I was coming to understand romance in an entirely new way—God's way. His idea of romance, I soon learned, was full of purity and innocence. It was the most fulfilling kind of romance that ever existed.

I had often dreamed of the moment my knight in shining armor would propose to me. I had envisioned all sorts of possible settings appropriate for this important event—a beautiful footbridge on a warm summer evening, overlooking a calm stream; an elegant, expensive restaurant over a sumptuous meal; or maybe riding in a white carriage through the brilliantly lighted streets downtown during the Christmas holidays.

No matter what the setting, I had determined these two things: I hoped it would be romantic, and I hoped my young suitor would find a way to surprise me. Though my mind was filled with endless dreams of how the night of my engagement would be, I never could have imagined anything close to the night Eric proposed to me.

"Kids, tomorrow night we are going to have a special dinner and have family pictures taken," Dad announced. "We're going to give Leslie a gift we've been waiting many years to give her."

My two younger brothers and I lifted our heads from the game we'd been playing on the living room floor.

"What is it?" we all questioned at once. My parents didn't often choose to surprise us, and stranger yet it was the middle of April—not at all close to any birthdays or Christmas.

My parents were nonchalant. "You'll see," was their only reply.

The next day was gloomy and overcast, yet there was a subtle excitement in the air. I spent the morning doing errands and the afternoon with a friend I hadn't seen in a while.

"I can't imagine what it could be," I told my friend after explaining to her what my parents had planned for that night.

"Well, maybe it's a new car," she offered hopefully.

A new car seemed a little farfetched, but I couldn't think of any other gift my parents would make such a big deal of so

I set my conclusion there. When I arrived home, my mom was busy preparing a nice meal in the kitchen. I offered to help.

"No, you need to go get ready. We're having pictures, so you need to get dressed up. Why don't you wear that new dress we just bought you?"

Shrugging, I went upstairs to get dressed. As I stood in the bathroom curling my long brown hair, my brothers came rushing up the stairs, laughing and pushing each other playfully as if they'd just heard some exhilarating news. I vaguely wondered what could have possibly gotten them so wound up.

When I had finished getting ready, I came downstairs to remarks from my family of how pretty I looked in my new dress. "Well, if it looks so good," I replied smiling, "I hope Eric does something special for me so I'll have another excuse to wear it!"

At this my brother, David, burst out laughing. I asked him what was so funny.

"Oh . . . you women," he stammered. "You're always thinking about clothes!"

After a delicious meal in the dining room, our family gathered in the living room for pictures. Then they took me into the adjoining room and told me to wait on the couch while they all went outside and got my gift.

"Now close your eyes," they instructed.

As I sat on the couch with my eyes closed, I heard the front door open and my family go outside. Meanwhile, a song started playing on the stereo. It was "How Beautiful."

"How special of my parents to think of playing this song! I'll have to call Eric tomorrow and tell him about it," I thought to myself as sentimental tears flowed from my closed eyes.

I heard footsteps in the hall but kept my eyes closed for the remainder of the song. When it had finally ended, there was a pause. I waited for my dad's voice to say, "OK, you can open your eyes!" The words never came. Instead, I heard Eric's voice softly whisper, "Leslie."

My eyes flew open. I gazed at him in complete shock. How did he get here? This was impossible—yet it was real.

The room had been transformed. The lights had been dimmed, candles lit, and flowers placed around creating a dream-like atmosphere. And there stood Eric with a handful of roses and a little white box. I knew the moment I had always dreamed of had finally arrived.

He did not speak, but as "Sunrise Song," a piano solo I had written, began playing on the stereo, he went to a basin of water that had been placed in the corner. Kneeling in front of me and weeping softly, he began to wash my feet. I knew what he was saying to me by this symbolic act. He was declaring his commitment to always be my servant—to lead me not closer to himself, but closer to Jesus. It was a moment unlike any other I have ever known. The air was thick with emotion.

The tape continued, perfectly timed to play songs that had been special between us at exactly the right moment. He recited to me a beautiful poem that he had written describing the life to which he had been called and beckoning me to join him. The last line was, "I ask you, my girl Leslie, will you marry me?"

I could not speak for a moment. Then, as the music crescendoed, I whispered a faint, "yes." The impact of what was happening had overwhelmed me.

Later I wondered how such a moment could feel so incredible when I had known for months that I would marry Eric. I realized the answer lay in the fact that we had given our emotions to God and had not allowed them to be released before it was time. Now, in God's perfect timing, He was releasing them, and they were more beautiful than ever. That night of our engagement was the first time Eric ever spoke the words "I love you" to me. He had been saving those words for the moment he would propose to his future wife, and what a priceless treasure they were.

Eric played for me a song he had written for the occasion, bringing tears to my eyes. When my parents and brothers came home (they had conveniently disappeared during all of this and had gone to get ice cream), Eric sang a song to my father that he had written years ago to the man who would one day give him the hand of his daughter. There was not a dry eye in the room. My father placed his hands on Eric and me. He blessed our engagement and prayed for us. It was beyond beautiful.

I had spent hours daydreaming of what the night of my engagement would be like, but none of my wildest romantic fantasies compared with this night. It was a gift from God, and each detail had been crafted by His hand. He had created the most romantic event I ever could have conceived—and all because we had chosen to do things His way.

Our friendship, engagement, and marriage have been laden with romance unlike any novel ever portrayed. I simply gave the area of relationship to God and determined to walk in purity, not knowing how He would bless me in return. As a result, I learned firsthand that God's way is the only way to experience pure romance!

# Eric, You May Now Kiss Your Bride!

### _____ Eric _____

I gently dipped my hands into the silver bowl. My fingers moist with water, I tenderly took her delicate foot and attempted to portray the humble Christ to her.

Leslie had reminded me over and over to be very careful with how much water I got onto my hands. "Just a little too much and it might drip on my dress," I heard her cute little concerned voice repeat time and time again.

Many people may have wondered why we would even include such an awkward and strange scene in our wedding ceremony. We knew why we did. As much hassle as it caused, it was worth it. We desired to express to each other and all the witnesses present the type of covenant we were making that day. It was more than a commitment to spend our lives together; it was a covenant to serve one another, purposing to lead each other unto Jesus Christ. Before Jesus proposed to His Bride with His very own body and blood, He washed His disciples' feet.

Washing feet has never been a glamorous act, but on this day, as I wetted and dried Leslie's feet, I found it to be a sparkling scene of romance. "I am your servant to lead you to your true Bridegroom," I told her as I slipped her white satin shoes back on.

The twirls and whirls of unquenchable expectation buzzed within my stomach as we stood and faced one another. Our feet were again in their normal habitat, but Leslie and I were in one we were truly unfamiliar with. The aura of excitement that encompassed the sanctuary seemed to paint a dream-like gloss upon every human movement.

An instrumental version of "How Beautiful" played in the background as the pastor stood beside us and asked us questions we had long before answered. "Yes! Yes!" my mind shouted. "Who wouldn't take this beautiful princess to be his wife?"

Our eyes tickled one another with the amazing love that coursed through our hearts, and our smiles seemed to light the darkened sanctuary with the joy of heaven. We knew very well what this covenant meant. It was unbreakable and for life . . . no matter what! Wild horses couldn't keep us from saying, "I will and I do!"

Three years ago, nearly to the day, I first laid eyes on this beautiful flower of God's. What an amazing work God had done! I surely was unworthy of such a treasure. "Almighty God," I thought, "You are faithful! You are truly faithful!" The rocks and pebbles I had placed in His nail-pierced hand had somehow become precious pearls. It was simply the work of a gracious and benevolent Father.

The pastor's voice seemed to sing as he led us in our vows and concluded with the powerfully profound words of Scripture, "What God has joined together let no man tear asunder." My heart fluttered and seemed to skip a beat as "the moment" finally came. The years we had awaited this moment seemed to join in chorus cheering us on. "Eric," the words harmonized in my heart, "you may now kiss your bride."

Never before had I met those rosebud lips. Oh, I'd longed to, but, boy, am I glad I waited until that electric moment. The heavens stood and erupted with a "Hallelujah!" and my heart seemed to burst like an alabaster jar of precious ointment. A great cheer came from the witnesses present. But Oh! they could not have known how wonderful it was. It was sensational!

"Hey, Les?" I whispered with an enormous smile on my face after the party had ended and we were alone. "If marriage is this good down here, what is it going to be like up in heaven?"

Leslie just giggled and shrugged and left it up to me to answer my unanswerable question. I surely don't claim to know what heaven will be like, but I *do* know it is going to be an awesome display of His extraordinary love . . . and His perfect faithfulness!

# After Thoughts . . .

Thank you for taking time to read our story! We hope it was an encouragement to you; for that is why it was written. In these final pages we want to further challenge you to travel the pathway of purity by addressing some commonly asked questions about this challenging area of relationships with the opposite sex.

We chose the title for this book, *His Perfect Faithfulness,* because we know that the miraculous way God brought us together was not based upon something we did on our own, but on God's great love for us as His children. We also know that our story is merely *one* example of His mighty hand at work in bringing a relationship together. We believe God wants to do something unique and special in this area of every young person's life.

It is one of our greatest desires to see young men and women purpose to live according to God's Word in relationships with the opposite sex. We know that when anyone gives this area of their life completely to Him, He will give back something beautiful.

If you have chosen to trust God in this area of your life, it is important to remember that your story will most likely turn out differently than ours because the Lord is so creative! However, we know when you look back and see His faithfulness to *you,* it will be the most perfect story you could ever have dreamed of. God will tailor-make your story to fit exactly with how He has created *you*!

While we know that God will not work the same way in everyone's life, we also believe that He has laid down certain principles in His Word for the area of relationships with the opposite sex. Principles such as internal and external purity, trusting in God, honoring authority, and waiting upon the Lord. These are not "the rules and regulations of courtship," but rather they outline a way of living for those who truly desire to give this area of their life to the Lord.

The motive for living according to these principles must be a sincere love for God and a deep desire to please Him. The strength to follow these principles must come from a daily, intimate relationship with the Savior. In any other setting they are empty and hollow and seem impossible to carry out; however, these principles applied in step with the Holy Spirit are truly life changing! The most important thing is *not* to follow a perfect formula. What matters is that you love Christ and seek to honor Him with all your heart, soul, mind, and strength.

If you have not surrendered to God in this area of your life, we pray that as you read this last portion of our book, you will be inspired to do so. We believe it is one of the most important decisions you can make in your Christian walk.

# Guy Talk

*D*ear Eric,

I know many young Christians, but I don't know *one* who's courageous enough to entrust this area of boy/girl relationships to God. I want to please God and I *do* want His best, but I feel I'm almost willing, in the case of relationships, to settle for second best and do it *my* way. Is that compromise? Help me, Buddy!

Your weak-kneed amigo,
Tim


*D*ear Tim,

Doesn't it just eat you up inside when you know what you ought to do but it just seems you can't take the step to do it? Tim, our generation doesn't need any more Christians who claim to live for Christ but inside have never surrendered to His Lordship.

When I was growing up, I intensely labored to dilute God's Word to meet my life and to affirm my actions, instead of lifting my thoughts and actions to meet the standard of His Word. I remember looking around me and measuring my virtue by comparing myself with my peers. I wasn't having sex, I wasn't taking drugs, and I wasn't drinking, but I lacked any backbone to uphold a standard any higher than that. When it came to risking popularity or to marring my reputation by standing up for Jesus, I refused to stand up and be counted.

The entire Israelite army shuddered with fear as a giant named Goliath boasted of his strength and invited a Hebrew challenger. It took just one young boy, who knew the power of his God, to take a stand, and the entire Israelite army gained confidence through his boldness.

Just like David, the shepherd boy, you are called to take a stand for what you know to be right. God will back you up! There were snickers as little David approached Goliath, but believe me, they stopped real quickly when God showed everyone who was boss. As a Christian, you must never play for the applause of this world, but play your very best for the smile of your King.

Our generation is in desperate need of examples in this area of relationship—ones who will take a stand for Jesus Christ and set their feet solidly upon His Word. We need courageous hearts who will lay all their desires for self-pleasure and self-serving popularity at Christ's feet and surrender to His plan for their lives.

Because I know you so well, Tim, I know your desire to serve God is greater than your desire to be liked by your peers. As young men, it's up to us to set the pace in showing sensitivity to women and treating them like the flowers God created them to be. It's our duty not to compare ourselves with the world but with the perfection of Jesus Christ. But it's only through a personal and intimate walk with the perfect Bridegroom that you and I, Tim, can become the gentle men God has called us to be.

Aim high with your standards, and bow low in humble obedience. God will grant you the strength and the grace to discover His very best.

Your brother in Christ,

Eric

ear Eric,

It's so encouraging to hear stories like yours, but after I put the book down and look in the mirror, I remember I'm a young man without someone to love like you're able to love Leslie. Sometimes I feel I'm not going to make it if I have to wait much longer. I feel like even though I may set my course for God's highest, I'm going to shipwreck somewhere in the Islands of Impatience, along the Shoreline of Discontentedness. How did you make it to twenty-three? I don't know if I can make it to eighteen!

Hurry up and answer,

Greg

*P*oor, poor Greggy!

I remember when God once showed me that the world is always in a hurry, but He teaches patience. Living in a micro-wavable fast-food society only makes it worse, doesn't it?

Imagine Moses waiting forty years on the back side of the desert! Or Abraham waiting over twenty years for his promised son, Isaac! Inconceivable? Not with God. But it *is* inconceivable without God.

There are two ways to wait: impatiently or contentedly. Contentment comes only when we know the One who is calling us to wait loves us and is faithful to His Word. If we don't know God is faithful and we are uncertain of His love for us, then naturally we will squirm as the clock ticks and there is still no sign.

There were many times I squirmed and squabbled with God as the years passed and there was still no sign of my wife. I panicked when I saw a gray hair sprouting out the side of my

71

head, wondering just how old God would allow me to be before He finally brought her into my life! It was only when I fell asleep in my love relationship with Christ that my anxieties subsided and my joy grew. It might seem like such a simple answer, but it is the essence of the Christian walk. When we focus on Christ, our concerns are pacified and all impossibilities are suddenly possible.

Each day it is so important for you to lay down your desires and pick up God's desires. Allow God to use this time of waiting to prepare you as a man. Not a grunting, hockey-loving, quiche-hating sort of a man, but an example of Christ Jesus. A man that is a model of His gentleness and humility, His mercy and His strength. These years of your life are fertile with opportunity to grow up in your faith and to learn how to lead your future family. You'll look back and truly cherish this time of development and thank God you didn't move in your own timing and your own way.

The rewards of impatience are here today and *gone* tomorrow. While patience may call us to sweat and tears, its rewards are not only of far greater magnificence, they never fade. They last for all time! Remember this little saying, Greg: "You can by the same grace that helped you through today, make it through tomorrow." Set your sails for the shores of heaven, and God will see to it you don't shipwreck!

Your crewmate,

*Eric*

*D*ear Eric,

Where did you find this girl? Okay, I know your answer; God found her for you. Eric, I would love to learn what it means to be a servant to my future wife, and I'd love to feel like I could cry in front of her like you did, but I honestly don't think in our culture there are other girls who would find that to be manly. In fact, I think it would be more viewed as weakness. I remember you in high school, so I know God has done this work in you, but I guess I'm struggling with allowing Him to do that tenderizing work in me. Speak to me, my fellow tough guy!

Ronny

*H*ey Ronny,

True manhood begins with the acknowledgment of weakness. It's in the soil of brokenness and humility that strength grows. God's "tough guys" are marked by uncompromising integrity and the true grit of unswerving loyalty to Truth.

I must correct you on your assumption of what girls in our culture find attractive. Sensitivity and tenderness will beat a dozen roses any day, and a listening ear and soft shoulder will outshine the clearest blue-diamond ring.

If God is desiring the very best for you, and you are willing to wait for her, she will be one that adores Christlikeness. The very best for you will be a woman who delights to see you pick up your Bible, who swoons when she hears you pray with conviction, who allows you to wash her feet and then freely lets you cry.

Whether you've ever seen a woman like that or not, I tell you, they're out there! Proverbs 31 (paraphrased) says, "Who can find them?" God can, Ronny. You wouldn't believe how many young women there are out there wondering the same thing. "Do young men really exist who reflect the tenderness of Christ, who walk confidently in His strength, and who dress in His humility and love?" Think about being the answer to that prayer.

Let God take you and mold you. He will fashion you into a heavenly "tough guy," a man who understands his emotions and is madly in love with Jesus Christ. One day someone will ask you, "Where did you find this girl?" You'll know the answer.

An aspiring tough-guy at your side,

*Eric*

*D*ear Eric,

I wish I'd read your book five years ago. Your relationship with Leslie is so special, so beautiful, but it is something I'll never be able to experience. Before I became a Christian I did not live a pure life. Is there any way God can redeem my past? Is there any hope for the future?

Anonymous

*D*ear Anonymous,

When you look at a caterpillar you can observe it in two ways. You can either say, "What an ugly creature! That's gross! Someone kill it!" Or you can say, "Isn't it amazing that such a homely creature can be transformed into such a lovely butterfly?" The second perspective is the way that God looks at us. When we come to Jesus, God doesn't look at us and see the ugliness of our sin anymore. Rather, He sees the beauty of the perfection of Christ.

So many of us come to Jesus for salvation but never realize the extent of what He did for us at the cross. He poured out His life's blood for us that we could be forgiven and made new!

In the book of Philippians Paul talks about forgetting what is behind him and pressing on to what is ahead (see 3:12-14). Both you and I can relate to that longing to have our past mistakes totally forgotten. But what we must learn to do is focus on what Christ is making us to be instead of on the mistakes we once made. When the question is an issue of, "Is there any hope?" the shout from heaven is, "Yes!"

To just consider the gospel message of Jesus Christ "good" news seems horrendously lacking. I think it would be better termed "unbelievably amazing" news! With Jesus, there is a glorious future. No matter what degree of sinfulness you have wallowed in, there is a future for you, bright and pure, washed clean by the blood of our Lord Jesus Christ.

When Christ's Spirit makes your heart His home, He doesn't complain about the mess you've made of it. He died because of that mess so that He could make you clean. He doesn't say, "Well this guy really blew it! I guess I won't be able to use him." He died for *all* of us who blew it. His objective when He sets up house is to make us like Himself and shine His perfection through us. He just loves to take a life that's wrecked and transform it into a picture of His great love.

You'd better believe it; you have hope! Jesus Christ, in His perfect faithfulness, is your living hope. We as His children are considered His workmanship. Once He's begun a work within us, He is faithful and more than capable to complete that work unto perfection. Our God is in the business of exchanging rags for riches.

Another ex-caterpillar,

*Eric*

*D*ear Eric,

No way! Impossible! I know myself too well. I know I couldn't make it to my wedding day before kissing my wife. In fact, I wouldn't even *want* to wait. Abstinence is hard enough, but *this* is plain ridiculous! Get real!

Jeff

*D*ear Jeff,

My thoughts exactly! I would have kicked and screamed the entire time if someone had told me I couldn't kiss Leslie until our wedding day. There is nothing that quenches the beauty of romance more than rules and regulations.

Just as there shouldn't be rules set up that force you to enjoy your favorite desert, there shouldn't be rules that *make* you enjoy the beauty of pure romance. When God fills you with His supernatural love, you don't need man's rules to tell you to do what pleases Him—you *want* to do what pleases Him.

As it says in Galatians 5, we've been set free! Does that mean freedom to do all those exciting things the world does? No way! It means something far different and far greater than that. It means that because of the work Christ did upon the cross, we're actually now free to live a life pleasing to God. Where before we knew Christ we were enslaved to our human passions, we are now at liberty to actually represent the very likeness of Jesus Christ through the way we live. We've been set free from man-made rules that tell us to "do this or that." We're now able to freely choose to bear the fruit of "love, joy, peace, patience, kindness, goodness, faithfulness, gentleness and self-control" (Galatians 5:22-23 NIV). Our entire life as Christians needs to be a reflection of this wondrous truth.

You should never be bound by Leslie's and my decisions in the area of our pre-marriage physical relationship. We did what we did because we felt that was what God was asking of *us*. We *wanted* to wait until marriage for our first kiss! We desired so much to do what would enhance our marriage in the years to come—not just gratify our temporal passions.

I'll never forget the amazing thrill of taking Leslie's hand when I proposed to her. It's a wonderful thing to express love through physical touch, but it also can be overpowering if not guarded by wisdom and self-control. A kiss, to you, might not seem like much, but let me tell you, wait three years for a kiss, and suddenly it's worth more than a treasure chest of gold.

Remember, Christ has set us free. You are not bound by rules; you are bound by the love of Christ. This love teaches us to forget *our* desires and embrace the desires of Christ. This love focuses on seeking the best for our future mate instead of seeking only what would feel good to us.

Choose, my friend, to stay pure because it's the way of love. Not just because Eric and Leslie did it that way, or because your parents want you to. God's ways may seem like insurmountable mountains, but He gives you the strength to climb them. What an amazing blessing is found at the peak. Keep trekking and you'll find out!

Aiming high,

*Eric*

# Girl Talk

ear Leslie,

I want to trust God with this area of my life, but all my friends are getting married, and I'm afraid I'll never meet someone. I'm not getting any younger, and I'm just not sure it's realistic for me to make a decision not to date. How will I meet someone? Can God really bring someone into my life if I'm not dating? Heidi

$\mathcal{D}$ear Heidi,

Your questions are so similar to the internal battle I went through a few years ago when I felt the Holy Spirit gently nudging me to turn this area over to God. It is so difficult to trust Him! I knew that God was asking me to give up dating, but it seemed so unrealistic to just sit around and wait for "prince charming" to come knocking on my door! I can definitely empathize with your struggle. But let me share with you a little conversation I had in my heart with the Lord when I was dealing with the same issues.

"Lord, I just *can't* stop dating! I'll never get married if I don't make myself available for young men to get to know me! People have always told me that 'the Lord can't steer a parked car.' It seems like irresponsibility on my part to just expect my husband to appear out of nowhere without any effort from me at all!"

"Leslie, do you believe that I have one special man picked out just for you, to be your husband?"

"Well, yes, I believe that, but . . ."

"Do you also believe that I am the God of all creation, and that I am perfectly capable of bringing your husband to you without your help?"

It *was* true! God didn't need my help. In fact, all my "help" thus far had only made a mess of things! The issue, I realized, was not if I believed God was able to bring my husband to me. The issue was if I could trust Him enough to take my hands off and let Him work in His perfect timing.

"Do you trust Me, Leslie? Do you truly trust Me?"

"Yes, Lord."

"Then show me with your life. It is one thing to say you trust Me, but it will only be *real* when you are finally willing to pry your hands loose from this area of your life."

It was intense! God was asking me to give up all control. I didn't like the feeling much at all! He was taking my hands off the steering wheel and asking me to sit in the back seat while He took over. I was afraid He wouldn't drive the car the way I wanted Him to. I was just sure the car would crash and burn. Reluctantly I moved to the back seat and closed my eyes with dread. Jesus took turns I never would have considered taking, yet they eventually brought me to the city of true joy. Looking back, it's clear that if I had kept driving down the same road I had been traveling without allowing Jesus to take over, *I* would have crashed and burned!

As the old hymn says, "Tis so sweet to trust in Jesus, just to take Him at His Word." Tears spring from my eyes even as I write those words. God's way *is* best!

Without dating, I knew that if I ever got married, it would be only because of a miraculous act of God. There was just no other way it could happen. And guess what! He did the impossible! He unfolded the most beautiful and romantic story I could have ever imagined—a relationship that never could have happened if I'd been doing things my way.

Whether you're sixteen or sixty, it makes no difference. God cares more about this area of your life than even *you* do; of this I have no doubt.

Keep trusting!

*Leslie*

*D*ear Leslie,

If I give up dating, how will I learn to relate to the opposite sex or to be prepared for marriage? How will I get to know the person God has chosen for me? How will I ever meet anyone?

Jenny

*D*ear Jenny,

When God first began stirring in my heart that I was to leave public high school and quit dating, I definitely panicked about the same questions you're asking. I pictured myself becoming a lonely, depressed teenager who did nothing all day but sit in a chair staring out the window with a forlorn expression. I thought the phone would never ring; I would never venture outside; and I would basically spend the rest of my teenage years as a hermit. What a dramatic change from the fun-loving, active girl I had always been! I wasn't sure I could handle it if I was going to have to live this way.

When I made the decision to leave high school, I did lose most of my friends and boys did stop calling me, but other things began to happen so quickly in my life that I hardly noticed. My relationship with my family grew stronger than it had ever been. Though I wouldn't have expected it, my family relationships actually began to prepare me for marriage!

I had often heard, "The way you treat your husband will be very similar to the way you treat your father and brothers." I learned to gain a servant's heart toward my dad and brothers and to communicate with them by trying to see things from their perspective. What better preparation for marriage than to first work on the relationships with the people who live with you?

Another thing God began to show me was the fact that just

because I was a teenager didn't mean I could have only teenage friends. In fact, He showed me how much I was missing out on by not having friends of all ages! I learned so much about communication and relating to people through the variety of adults and children I became friends with.

Through those relationships, I also began to meet other young people. I began to have true friendships with young men, free from ulterior motives. In high school with my "flirting" boy/girl relationships, I had never learned how to be myself with the opposite sex or felt comfortable around guys. Now that I finally had true friendships with these godly young men, based upon our love for Christ, I was being educated on how to relate to them! It was amazing how God brought young men out of the woodwork for me to be friends with when I wasn't even seeking out relationships! I learned far more about relating to the opposite sex *after* I gave up dating than before.

You'll be surprised how many other young people God is raising up who have these same convictions. I never dreamed that after making this commitment not to date, I would become friends with at least four or five godly young men who felt the same way I did about dating! God has a way of supernaturally bringing like-minded people together. If you step back and patiently allow Him to orchestrate your friendships, you'll be amazed at what happens.

Look around at your family and all the other people in your life right now, young and old. By simply challenging yourself to deepen your relationships with them, you find one of the best preparations for marriage you could ever have!

As for the fear of never meeting someone—trust God. He is a master at weaving together relationships. He can do what seems impossible anytime He wants. Keep your eyes upon Him, Jenny, and I know He will be faithful to you.

Remain in Him!

*Leslie*

ear Leslie,

I have made the decision not to date and to allow God to bring my future husband to me in His time, but I still have a hard time keeping my emotions towards guys under control. I want Christ to be my first love, but I feel so distracted by these thoughts and feelings. Help!

Sarah

*D*ear Sarah,

I'll let you in on a secret I learned a few years ago: it is impossible for anyone to control emotions! In your own strength you simply cannot do it. That's why surrendering your emotions to God is the key to inward purity. Giving the area of relationships to God, even giving up dating, is of little value if you are constantly running after relationships in your mind.

Surrendering your emotions to God is something that must go beyond the initial decision to stop dating and to start trusting Him with this area of your life; it is a daily commitment that requires sacrifice. If you are not living in a personal, intimate, daily walk with Christ, it will be impossible to carry out your commitment.

It is easy, as a young girl, to start carelessly daydreaming about different guys and to let yourself have romantic feelings towards them. Pretty soon you find yourself going out of your way to be around them, trying to get their attention by talking with them or flirting with them. Soon your whole life revolves around the way the guy treats you. He becomes the center of your entire world. He is all you can think about, and thoughts of him crowd out everything else. This is so dangerous! It crowds out God and all that is important, and it ends only in heartache.

You must stop the process of giving away emotions before it ever starts. The Bible, in 2 Corinthians 10:5 (NASB), reveals the secret of stopping emotions before they start. God tells us to take "every thought captive to the obedience of Christ."

Learn to catch thoughts toward guys the moment they enter your mind. Ask yourself if the thoughts are glorifying to God or if your future husband would feel comfortable if he knew the thoughts you are entertaining right now. Daydreaming about young men seems so innocent, but the emotional roller coaster it leads you on ends by crashing and burning. Refuse to *dwell* upon thoughts about young men. This does not mean you should never think about guys, but be careful not to let those thoughts dominate your mind or control your actions. You can memorize Scripture to meditate on when you are tempted.

Most of all, make your relationship with Him your *focus* through daily quiet times of reading His Word. Here are some suggestions to help you grow in intimacy with Him: Keep a journal of prayers and of all He is teaching you. Write about all the little things you learn about Him each day. Look for ways to serve others. Read biographies of Christian women of the past to be inspired by their walk with God.

A good goal is to become so consumed in your relationship with the Lord that giving your emotions to guys isn't as much of a temptation. Not that the struggle will completely disappear, but the stronger your relationship with Christ is, the less of a distraction your emotions will be.

Christ will not become your first love simply through wishful thinking. It takes a daily, active relationship with Him, a daily commitment to surrender your life into His hands. Don't try to do it in your own strength. He's right there, Sarah, ready to help you all the way!

He is faithful!

*Leslie*

*D*ear Leslie,

I love your story and so desire the same work of God in my own life, but I have a nagging worry: "What if God wants me to remain single?" Nothing sounds worse; I don't know if I could handle it!

Annette

*D*ear Annette,

It wasn't until I gave this area of my life to God that I dealt with the fear of remaining single. Without dating I knew that this area of my life was totally dependent upon God, and I was so worried that He wanted to take me through the fiery trial of lifelong singleness! One day I read a verse in the Bible that helped me overcome my fear in this area. "Delight yourself in the Lord; and He will give you the desires of your heart" (Psalm 37:4 NASB). Ponder that for a moment. The more you become like Christ, the more your desires become intertwined with His desires. He actually places *His* desires within your heart!

I saw that the desire I had in my heart to get married was most likely placed there by God! This gave me tremendous relief for I realized that as long as I was growing in my relationship with Christ and truly seeking His will, He would mold the desires of my heart to fit perfectly with His plan for my life. Even if His plan for me *did* turn out to be singleness, I had confidence that He would change my heart to *desire* to be single.

My mom once told me of a conversation that changed her life. She knew a godly woman in her church who had lost a son in a car accident. My mom was dealing with worry over her children, dreading the thought of anything ever happening to one of us. Finally she asked this woman how she ever made it through such a tragic experience. The woman replied, "God gives you the grace to go through difficult times when you need it, and not before." My mom realized that although she couldn't imagine making it through the trauma of such an experience, God's grace would be poured out upon her to help her through if anything ever did happen to one of her children. This gave her freedom from years of worry.

The same principle is true for your worry about remaining single. Though it is something you can't imagine being able to handle now, know that if it is God's plan for your life, His grace will be sufficient for you! The key is to stay close to Him, Annette. He will not take you through circumstances you will be unable to bear.

You also need to realize that God's plans for you, as His child, are for good! Jeremiah 29:11 (TLB) says, "For I know the plans I have for you . . . plans for good and not for evil, to give you a future and a hope." Don't look at God as some big old meanie up in heaven just delighting Himself in your misery. He wants so much for you to experience true joy! He is a loving Father who cares more about this area of your life than even you do. Trust that His plans for you are beyond what you can even imagine. "No eye has seen, no ear has heard, nor has it entered into the heart of man what God has prepared for those who love Him" (1 Corinthians 2:9 NIV).

If you truly have a desire in your heart to get married, most likely that desire is from God and He wants to fulfill it in His perfect time. Just make sure you stay willing for Him to change your desires. He is so gentle with His children!

Rest in His love for you, Annette; He has only your very highest in mind.

Keep your eyes on Jesus,

*Leslie*

*D*ear Leslie,

Hardly any boys have shown an interest in me. I don't find myself attractive at all, and I honestly don't think anyone would ever want to marry me. Giving up dating is one thing, but what about when no one wants to date you in the first place? Will I ever get married at this rate?

Angie

*D*ear Angie,

It may surprise you to know you are not the only one who has this concern. Thousands of young people feel the exact same way! The enemy has brainwashed our society to believe a lie in this area of self-worth. He has deceived so many of us into assuming we are not valuable or attractive simply because we don't look like Barbie.

Our society has defined "beauty" in its own way. If you don't look like the cover of a magazine, you are not considered beautiful. The media constantly reminds those of us who do not fall into their category of beautiful that we are not attractive. As children and teenagers, we are conditioned to be attracted only to what our society considers pleasing to look at. But we can't base our opinion of our beauty upon society's guidelines!

I'll never forget my surprise when I went to Mexico and found out that in their culture fair skin, rather than tan, was considered beautiful. For years I had felt bad that my fair skin never seemed to tan the way all my friends' did. The Mexicans thought it absurd that Americans actually paid to lie in tanning booths to make themselves darker. They wanted to make themselves as light skinned as possible! What foolish lengths we go to in order to try and look like the latest picture of perfection.

God's ways are bigger than the world's silly ideas of beauty. He made everyone with a unique attraction gift. If it is God's will for you to be married, He has also chosen someone very special just for you. This young man was created to blend with your life, your calling, your gifts, and your personality. Even more amazing, this man will have an attraction gift that will fit perfectly with who you are. He will find you absolutely beautiful in every way. Just as Adam was fully enraptured by Eve, so your husband will be by you.

It's also important to remember that God puts far more value on our internal beauty, which comes from a heart that is fully His, than external beauty, which fades so quickly (Proverbs 31:30).

It's amazing how much a joyful, radiant spirit affects a person's external appearance. The more you focus on preserving your internal beauty by purity of life and thought, the more your external appearance will soften and glow. Internal beauty will stand the test of time and eventually present you with a crown of glory, while beauty on the outside is temporary and of little value.

No matter what society has made you think of yourself, God considers you beautiful and valuable. He created you just the way He wanted you! You are so precious in His sight! You are His princess, His treasured child. He loves you more than you are even capable of comprehending. Always remember that God values a heart that fears the Lord far more than outward good looks. If His plan for you is marriage, He has created a man who will love everything about you. So while you wait, focus on adorning your heart and not just your outward appearance. A quiet and gentle spirit is of unfading beauty (1 Peter 3:4).

With confidence in Him,

*Leslie*

*D*ear Leslie,

It's great the way your parents were so involved in your relationship with Eric, but my parents wouldn't be that cool about it. They are so protective of me; they don't want me to grow up. If I tried to honor them by letting them be involved in this area of my life, I just know they'd walk all over me!

Jessica

*D*ear Jessica,

"Honor your father and your mother . . . that it may go well with you," the Bible says (Ephesians 6:1-2 NIV). This doesn't mean just tolerating them, but embracing and accepting the spiritual authority God has given them over our lives. He puts our parents over us for our spiritual, emotional, and physical protection.

As a teenager, when I felt crowded by my parents, I first handled it by drawing away from them. Though it seemed like the logical thing to do, it only made the situation worse. Because I was no longer open with them, they found it harder to trust me and became more restrictive in what they would allow me to do. When I did not resist their protectiveness but cheerfully submitted to them, it seemed to cause them to respect my maturity and grant me more freedom to make my own decisions.

If you are truly honoring them and involving them in your life, chances are they will notice your maturity and back off a little. If they remain overprotective, however, there are ways you can deal with this other than withdrawing from them.

First of all, pray! God is able to change their hearts and show them where they are wrong. But begin with yourself. Ask God to show you anything in your attitude that is not pleasing to Him. Then ask Him to help your parents to see you as a mature young person.

After giving this area to God, it might help to speak to them, but only in a proper way. Do not do it when you are frustrated with them. You can too easily say things you'll regret in the heat of emotion. Wait for the right moment when all of you are calm. Don't accuse them. Just share your concern in a gentle, loving way. Give them practical examples of how they can begin to allow you to grow up. Be sure to let them know how much you appreciate their loving concern. You'll be surprised at what kind of results this respectful attitude can produce!

It's necessary for me to add here that not all young people are blessed with God-fearing parents. If your parents are non-Christians, does that exclude you from the obligation to honor them? God does not make exception for this in the Bible; He simply commands us to honor our parents. You need to honor their *position* in your life, not necessarily their character. This might mean just simple things like respecting their rules of what time to be home or when to do your homework. Or maybe offering to help around the house. What about showing respect for them in your tone of voice? If you are diligent in this, you might even one day find that they are won over to Christ by your consistent, respectful behavior!

If your parents are close to the Lord, you have a unique and wonderful opportunity to see God work through them in this area of your life. If they are not, you still can't go wrong in choosing to honor them. They may not be perfect or even good parents, but God can show you ways to respect them. Examine your heart. Do you honor your parents in the little, everyday things of life? Do you listen to them? Do you value the wisdom they have? Do you express your love for them? Do you appreciate all they've done for you, and do you show them gratitude?

Honoring your parents is not a dismal duty. Try it and you'll find it to be one of the most rewarding decisions you ever make!

In His unfailing love,

*Leslie*

$\mathcal{D}$ear Leslie,

Your story is a beautiful ideal, but as I look around at the way young people today are living, it seems hopeless that this could ever be the standard for forming relationships. Do you think it is really possible for teenagers who are so embroiled in the dating scene to give it all up and learn to live in true purity?

Stacey

$\mathcal{D}$ear Stacey,

As I was praying about your question, I felt God reminding me of a time a few years ago when I was first asked to share my convictions on purity with a youth group filled with young people who were "walking the fence." I, too, experienced a deep sense of hopelessness as I observed their lives.

They were kids who had to walk into a living hell each day, surrounded on every side by evil forces that lured them into compromise. They wanted to live the Christian life, but they didn't know an alternative to the dating scene which only sent them plunging down the wrong path. Their parents, assuming things to be pretty much the same as when *they* were young, allowed and even encouraged them to date at early ages, unaware of the horrors they were permitting to come upon their precious children. Even most of the Christian environments they were in, such as youth groups or camps, encouraged and catered to boy/girl relationships. No matter where they were, they were not considered "normal" unless they had "someone."

The compromise they were living in was a perfect picture of how most Christian youth today live. They know in their hearts what is right, but when it comes down to sacrificing their pride or popularity, sin usually wins out.

When I see kids like this, I literally *feel* the pain, the searching, the pressure! I know exactly what each one of those teenagers has to face every day of their lives, how difficult it is to make the right decisions, how easy it is to fall . . . because I was there. I went through it. And I fell. I made wrong choices which I can never revoke.

Yes, Stacey, I can understand why you would question the probability of kids in this intense struggle actually turning and walking a totally different way. Is there hope? I must admit I have asked myself the same question more than a few times. It looks like an impossible situation. But I know it is not. Remember, I was there! I believed then, and I still hold to it now, that if I'd just seen *one* example of someone who walked in purity, just *one* person who went another way, I would have been strong enough to be the second. I would have been spared years of heartache and deep regret over wrong choices. Countless other lives could have been changed if I had responded to God's call to take a stand for Him.

It wasn't until much of my youth had been wasted that I gained the proper perspective and decided to walk another way. I feel that God is now calling me to be the example I wasn't while in public high school—one who stands in the midst of hurting peers and beckons them to rise to a standard of true purity. All He needs are those few who are willing to step out and be the first example. There are so many young people who are inwardly crying out for another way. Though it often may seem hopeless, I believe that many times all they need is to be challenged to rise above the common standard.

If you are that first example, others will follow in your footsteps. Even if, for a time, it seems you are all alone, there is no doubt that your obedience will touch many lives in due time. Rise up and be that one, Stacey, and trust that with God nothing is impossible!

For the sake of the call,

*Leslie*

# Straight Talk

# To Date or Not to Date –
# Is That Really the Question???

Let us answer this question by asking you a question. Is Jesus Christ the greatest love of your life? Just pause for a second and think about it. Do you love Jesus more than your music? Or how about your sports? What about your reputation? Do you adore Jesus more than every other thing in your life? Do your friends hold a tighter reign on your heart than the King of Kings? Does your passion for pleasure have a greater priority in your life than knowing that God is pleased with you?

If Jesus does not hold such a place of mastery over your heart and life, then the place to begin is *not* bowing your head and praying for your future mate. It is bowing your heart and falling at your *rightful* King's feet and asking forgiveness.

Our challenge to you is not to give up dating; we challenge you rather to give your entire heart to Jesus Christ. Give Him His worthy place of Lordship—not only in the area of relationships with the opposite sex, but in every area. When Jesus becomes the Lord of your life, the question transforms from, "What's wrong with dating?" to "Lord, how can I please You in this area of my life?" When He is Lord, it's amazing, but you stop the groaning over the seeming restrictions God places over your life, and you start rejoicing in the opportunity to be an example of Him for all the world to see. When your heart is God's, your life is destined to a magnificent display of His faithfulness.

It must be understood that the real weakness of dating is *not* its potential for heartache but the fact that it robs God of His place. His place is that of a Father, a Shepherd, a Counselor, and a Friend. If He is the One who is to lead us in our every decision in this life, why should this all-important area be an exception?

Just imagine your life as if it were a great drama. The entire heavens curiously watch with rapt attention to see how this great drama will unfold. What an opportunity you have to display the perfect faithfulness of God through your life, but if Jesus Christ is not the lone author and director of your great drama, the story will never be used to the praise of the glory of His awesome grace.

*If you do not yet know Jesus Christ as your Lord and Savior, may we have the honor of introducing you . . .*

**Beware:** Once you meet the King of the Universe, you'll never be the same.

Choices . . . There are just so many choices to make in this life. If you don't feel like that's true for you, just wait a few years. Each decision must be weighed on the scale of positive and negative implications.

Jumping out of moving cars is a choice we choose *not* to make due to the ill effects it has upon the human body. Yet the opposite is true when we talk about the choice to get dressed in the morning. We may not particularly enjoy the selection of outfits in our closet, but we undoubtedly still choose to get dressed due to the ill effects it would have upon our reputation if we did not.

Most people treat surrendering their life to Jesus Christ as if it were another one of those choices in life. They weigh it on their scale and determine its ill effects as opposed to its positive features and decide accordingly. "It's just not very conducive to my popularity," some may say. Others might reason, "There's so much of life to live yet. I'll do that when I get to be an old fogey and there's nothing worth living for anymore." Even others are bold enough to exclaim, "I don't need Jesus! I'm doing just fine on my own."

Whoa! Hold on there! If any thoughts of this kind have been passing through your mind, it's very important that you listen up. Choices are undoubtedly a wonderful gift from God. We are certainly not robots without a free will of our own. But surrendering your life to Jesus Christ is *not* just another choice with temporary significance. It is a divine command to us as humans from the very Creator of the universe. It still may be considered a choice, but it consists of either siding with God eternally or siding against God eternally. Quite a choice, huh? Especially when you understand the ramifications of siding against God.

It is one of the most basic principles laid out in the Bible that we, as humans, are totally in need of God for salvation. In other words, no matter how many good things we do in this life, no matter how nice we are, no matter how many times we even attend church, without the intervention and help of God we will never make it to heaven. In fact, without the supernatural aid of God, we're actually doomed for eternity in hell.

You may say, "That's not fair! If I'm a good person, then God will surely not just send me to hell. I thought you said He was loving?"

Oh, He's loving all right! You see, according to God's Word we are all born sinners. There just isn't such a thing as a "good" person outside of God. We all have a natural desire to oppose God and to be gods ourselves. It says in Romans 3:23 (NIV), "All have sinned and fall short of the glory of God." The consequence of this sin is death. (This is where the love comes in.) God can have nothing to do with sin; it's totally opposed to who He is. Because He loved us so very much, He took the consequences of our sin upon Himself. He did that by sending His Son, Jesus, to die in our place. God literally walked this earth clothed in our humanity with the sole purpose of laying down His life and suffering for our sin. The punishment we deserved He took upon Himself. When He had accomplished this work through His death, He then, by God's mighty Spirit, was raised from the dead.

We now have a means of finding salvation. In the Bible it's termed a "narrow door." That narrow door is Jesus Christ and Jesus Christ alone. Narrow, means there's only *one* way. It is entered through believing in the finished work of Jesus Christ upon the cross and surrendering to His Lordship and rule in your life.

You see, turning to Christ is the *only* way to be right with God. So many other religions have their ways and formulas. They are utterly sincere in practicing them, but in the end their sincerity will not save them. The cross is the only gate by which we can enter the path that leads to eternal life. Forgiveness is available only through the blood of Jesus Christ.

"Well," you say, "how can I come to God and gain this salvation?"

God is so enormous that our minds cannot come close to comprehending His magnificence. God is so pure and so glorious that if we were to look upon Him in all His brilliance, we probably would die instantly. Yet this huge and powerful God has become real and personal to us through Jesus. With open arms He waits for us to come to Him. We discover this infinite God to be so wonderfully tender and so quick to forgive us of our many mistakes. Though He is so majestic and indescribably awesome, He takes delights in us. We are so tiny and so seemingly insignificant, but He longs to share in relationship with us. He loves when we speak to Him and express to Him our feelings and our questions. He knows our every thought, but He still cherishes our communication as a father does a child's.

If you are sensing Jesus beckoning you this day to come to Him, just know that He is ready to forgive if you are ready to acknowledge your need for forgiveness. To express this heart desire to God, maybe you would like to pray something like this:

Dear Jesus, I am so grateful for what You have done for me even though I am so undeserving of Your grace. I confess that I have sinned against You and have not submitted to Your rightful rule over my life. Please forgive me for my sins against You. I surrender my life to You today and acknowledge You as my Savior, my Lord, and my King. I am certainly not worthy of Your kindness. Take my life from this day forward and let it be forever used to bring praise to Your Name.

Jesus Christ is worthy of your life. He gave everything for you; the very least you can do is offer Him your life of obedience in return.

Choose this day to come to Jesus for He has already chosen you. He calls you this day to follow Him. Lay your life in His strong and tender hands as a piece of clay does in a potter's. Quit trying to mold yourself. Allow Him to masterfully and lovingly shape you. Beware, though, when you come to know Jesus, you will be forever spoiled for just an ordinary life. You will be compelled to live a life of selfless love. And when you come to know Jesus, you will finally discover *His Perfect Faithfulness* in your life.

There's no more introduction necessary. If you do not yet know Jesus Christ as your Lord and Savior, there's no better time than the present. ✝

# Special Note . . .

We sincerely hope this story was an encouragement to you as a testimony of God's faithfulness. We are so excited about what He has done in our lives and feel privileged to be able to share this story with others!

If you would like information on how to obtain additional copies of *His Perfect Faithfulness*, please contact:

> Family Foundations Publishing
> P. O. Box 320
> Littleton, CO 80160
> (303) 797-1139

If you are interested in scheduling us to speak or sing at your church, conference, or other function, please contact:

> Eric and Leslie Ludy
> (in care of Rich and Janet Runkles)
> 2130 Ridgeview Way
> Longmont, CO 80501
> (303) 651-9530

If we can serve you in any way through prayer, counsel, or encouragement, please don't hesitate to write or call us at the above location. We would love to hear from you! May God bless you as you continue to seek and follow Him!

> Sincerely,
>
> *Eric & Leslie*

To request a free catalog of books and tapes
with similar subject matter,
please write:

**Family Foundations Publishing**
PO Box 320
Littleton, CO 80160